COLLECTED POEMS OF JOHN WHEELWRIGHT

COLLECTED POEMS

OF

JOHN WHEELWRIGHT

Edited by
ALVIN H. ROSENFELD

with an introduction by
AUSTIN WARREN

A NEW DIRECTIONS BOOK

ACKNOWLEDGEMENTS

The following poems appeared in *The Southern Review* (Spring 1971): "Talk with Robert Hillyer," "More Straitly Than a Vow," "D'Autre Temps," "A Twin Toilet, After
Rowlandson," "Cathedral," "A Poem by David McCord."

Published simultaneously in Canada by McClelland & Stewart, Ltd.
Printed in Italy

New Directions Books are published by James Laughlin by New Directions Publishing
Corporation, 333 Sixth Avenue, New York 10014

CONTENTS

PORTRAIT

To place the precisely slippered toes
With meditation on each stair;
To hold his lurking counterpose
Of anger, smiling to play fair;

To balance with his glittering sea-
Eyes the fragility of bone,
Slender and gaunt as a winter tree—
Studied all grace, and so his own.

To be cat-eyed, slit-eyed, to catch
Astringent nets of namby creatures,
That with articulate despatch
He skewered with their pamby teachers;

To note in the cold Boston bay
The flouncing light on the clean arches;
To know with exact hate the way
A faking builder stuffs and starches;

To stand amid his Where and Whence
With verse in never-ending bout,
To figure some unworldly sense
And keep the melodic nonsense out;

To write a sterner myth than Tate's
Or that of Cummings or of Crane—
Owned and disowned the Concord gates
And Cousin Brooks' sweet terrain.

But saw the heads of death that rode
Within each scoundrel's limousine,
Grinning at hunger on the road
To incorporate the class machine;

vii

And saw the tower of the poor,
Lonely, ignoble, noisy, blind,
With that great Cross upon the tower.
Fantasy drove him out of mind.

Yet upward in LaFarge's flame
His saviour twisted, and does still;
The true line comes as once it came
To masculine Homer's steady will;

Control and Charity of the just,
And their wild laughter flung at night,
Commemorate his death, his dust,
His gaiety. John Wheelwright.

Robert Fitzgerald

PREFACE

John Wheelwright had published three collections of poetry—*Rock and Shell* (1933), *Mirrors of Venus* (1938), and *Political Self-Portrait* (1940)—when, in September of 1940, he was struck and killed by a drunken driver in his native Boston. At the time he was preparing the manuscript of his fourth collection, to be called "Dusk to Dusk," which had progressed far enough toward publication for the poet to announce it as "forthcoming" in his latest book.

But John Wheelwright was not to live to see his new book to press, nor was his literary executor successful, despite attempts, in having it appear. Thereafter the manuscript of "Dusk to Dusk" was put away and virtually forgotten. It was only recently recovered and appears here for the first time, together with the complete texts of Wheelwright's three previously published collections and a section of "Additional Poems" never before collected or published by the poet.

With only few exceptions, the poems of the three earlier books—all now scarce—appear here without change. The most significant alteration is in the poem "The Inception of the Cross" (*Rock and Shell*), which, in line 39, originally printed "eclipse" for "ellipse." The poet himself calls attention to this error in the Argument to "Dusk to Dusk," and it has now been corrected; a few other typographical errors have likewise been corrected.

Otherwise, the present text reproduces the poems of *Rock and Shell*, *Mirrors of Venus*, and *Political Self-Portrait* as they appeared when those volumes were first published. There is evidence that John Wheelwright read and corrected his own proof sheets for these books, and the assumption is, therefore, that the poetry was as he wanted it, even with regard to the occasionally unusual punctuation, which has not been altered here.

The manuscript of "Dusk to Dusk," on the other hand, was not yet finalized and lacked authorized texts of "Masque with Clowns" (here reprinted from Wheelwright's pamphlet, *Poems for a Dime*), "The Dark before the Day," "Evening," "Morning," and the Argument, which have been supplied from working copies. The final

ix

text of "The Other," which Wheelwright read to Howard Blake and Austin Warren on September 12, 1940, apparently disappeared in the automobile accident, but it has been reconstructed from working copies. Wherever possible, misprints in the typescript have been corrected from other copies; some repunctuation has been necessary; and, in all instances, the last manuscript changes have been incorporated.

The "Additional Poems" include three pieces reprinted from *Diogenes* (December 1940 / January 1941) and one from *Fantasy* (1940, no. 4). Wheelwright had revised for publication five poems from *Eight More Harvard Poets* (1923), and these are also included; the other five had already been incorporated in published poems. Several short poems found among the manuscripts are here printed for the first time.

Another first appearance in the "Additional Poems" is the section from "Blackstone and Appleseed," a long poem that Wheelwright was working on at the time of his death and one which he had apparently planned as a book-length work. In one of the front leaves of *Political Self-Portrait* the poem was announced as "in preparation," and it is particularly unfortunate that the poet did not live to complete it, for it surely would have been one of his most interesting. The poem seems to have been planned along the lines of an American mock-epic, with some of the grandeur of conception of Walt Whitman tempered and deflated by the wryness and moral indignation of a New England descendant of Emerson and Thoreau. Wheelwright's gift for rendering the accents of colloquial New England speech is prominently displayed in the easy lines of "Blackstone and Appleseed," and the amusing figure of Blackstone—something of a poetic picaro, weaving in and out of the various sections—would have helped to make this a very attractive poem. Although only a small section of "Blackstone and Appleseed" has been found, then, it nonetheless has been deemed worthy enough as an example of Wheelwright's late work to be included here.

Wheelwright was also laying out another long poem about Thomas, his favorite saint, but that has been deemed too fragmentary for publication. It opens with the flight of the apostle from the fatal marriage in "Twilight" (*Rock and Shell*) to the city of man-eaters, which is evidently the world of business. Here a slave is purchased for thirty pieces of silver, to build for Gundaphores, king of India, a palace based on "the simple volumes of geometry." Wheelwright's skeleton of the plot reads: "Christ buys Thomas from Antichrist. Christ goes in boat with Thomas. Thomas preaches to Christ. Thomas learns Christ. Antichrist shows him bill of sale. Christ exacts Thomas from Antichrist, and gives Thomas bill of sale."

S. Foster Damon was personally responsible for the survival of the major part of Wheelwright's manuscripts after the poet's death, including the manuscript of "Dusk to Dusk." His devotion to his brother-in-law and friend is reflected in the dedication to his own *The Moulton Tragedy* (1970): "to John Wheelwright poet and brother."

Austin Warren has kindly revised his essay on John Wheelwright, which appears in his *New England Saints* (1956). It is reprinted here with the permission of The University of Michigan Press.

Robert Fitzgerald has permitted the reprinting of his memorial poem, "Portrait," which is to be found in his collection *Spring Shade* (New Directions, 1971).

There is yet no biography of John Wheelwright, but readers will learn much from Matthew Josephson's recent essay, "Improper Bostonian: John Wheelwright and His Poetry," in *The Southern Review* (Spring 1971).

Louise Wheelwright Damon, the poet's surviving sister, has been of help in countless ways.

Special thanks are due to Mrs. Christine Hathaway, Special Collections Librarian at Brown University, where most of the Wheelwright manuscripts are housed, and to her staff. I am likewise grateful to K. C. Gay, Curator of the Poetry Collection, Lockwood Memorial Library, State University of New York at Buffalo.

Thanks are also due to numerous friends of the Wheelwright family who have helped make this publication possible: John Nicholas Brown, Charles Henry Coster, Mrs. Christina Sedgwick Marquand, Oliver Prescott, Thomas E. Proctor, Jr., George Roberts, Miss Susan Street, and Mr. and Mrs. James B. Thayer.

The editor is grateful to Indiana University, which awarded him a Faculty Fellowship for the summer of 1970 to pursue research for this book.

ALVIN H. ROSENFELD
Indiana University

Introduction: JOHN BROOKS WHEELWRIGHT

Wheelwright was of Boston as Thoreau of Concord. Bostonwise, though he knew his Europe—the Paris of Hemingway and Fitzgerald —he had never traveled farther west than Albany. But he had traveled much in Boston—from the Somerset Club and the Hill to the South End.

When, in 1940, a speeding truck killed this irreplaceable American, his friends, who had taken for granted that good old Jack would go on being his unpredictably amusing, exciting self, were left with an unpredictable sense that what was lost was not—now that time for diagnosis had come—so peripheral: that he was a serious, meticulous poet; not a minor wit but a master of metaphysical poetry.

For long, "Wheels" had been one of Boston's spectacular *divertisse-ments*. He was the current representation of its wit and audacity—the apostolic successor to Mrs. Jack Gardner and Amy Lowell, Father Van Allen of the Anglo-Catholic Church of the Advent, and H.T. Parker, music critic for the *Transcript* and sole male resident of the Hotel Vêndome.

His lineage was symptomatic, symbolic. On his father's side he was descended from the Reverend John Wheelwright, a Puritan who fled Laudian England in 1636, only to encounter the stringencies of theocratic Massachusetts Bay. Though a Calvinist, he was a strong advocate for freedom of religious opinion, a zealous backer of the Antinomian Anne Hutchinson, who accused most of the clergy of teaching the Covenant of Works, not of Grace. In 1636-37, Wheelwright was the preacher at the Fast Day of the Boston Church; in consequence, Governor Winthrop and the General Court summoned him before them, pronounced him "guilty of sedition and contempt," and banished him and his friends from the Colony. It is he who is invoked in "Bread-Word Giver" as ancestor of rebels and anarchists and reformers and other "enthusiasts," whom New England has never lacked—from Williams to Alcott and Garrison and the Adamses to Sacco and Vanzetti and Robert Lowell—and of whom "Wheels" claimed membership by birthright.

Saint, whose name and business I bear with me;
rebel New England's rebel against dominion;
who made bread-giving words for bread makers;
whose blood floods me with purgatorial fire;
I, and my unliving son, adjure you:
keep us alive with your ghostly disputation
make our renunciation of dominion
mark not the escape, but the permanent of rebellion.

On his mother's side, there was political power and wealth. John Brooks was governor of Massachusetts from 1817 to 1822, six terms. His second cousin, Peter Chardon Brooks (1767-1849) built, through money from the East India trade, a mansion at Medford. At his death in 1849, he was reputed to be the richest man in New England. Brooks's estate in West Medford boasted a garden that "Wheels" (which, as symbolically dialectical, he liked to style himself) calls in the note to "Paul and Virginia," "the most splendid of Massachusetts, where the author spent the summers of early childhood."

The Brookses were not Jack's sole claim to grandeur. "Footsteps" is alleged—with what warrant I don't know—to be, in style, a continuation of "Alexander's Feast" by "the Author's seventeenth century kinsman, John Dryden." And in the Argument (that is, notes) to the same volume, *Political Self-Portrait*—the last published and the most radical—the second stanza of "In Poets' Defence" is affirmed to take its origin from "an oration by that flower of New England [a choice specimen of double talk, that phrase], the Author's mother's father's uncle by marriage, the Honorable Edward Everett."

Like all "proper Bostonians," Jack derived from the proper marriages of "mind" on the one side and, on the other, money and social correctness. Both sides have their "claims" and their rewards. Jack was duly aware of being, in his own person, both a "gentleman" and also an Independent. But, clearly, it was the line of the "Bread-Word Giver" which, so far as he could, he chose. He first showed his rebellion by a series of adolescent pranks calculated to shock his own social class, Bostonly ruled by decorous women, and to the end of his days he felt it one of his duties to be an authorized shocker, a conscientious violator of all genteel refinements. To assure himself that he was being candid, he had to surrender all fear of being taken for rude. If he liked, he took a nap on a park bench; forced his citizen's way into the Ritz of the Vêndome unclad in the ritual garments; at restaurants banged with knife and fork upon his table till the waiter had corrected an order carelessly heard or imperfectly prepared.

Since he followed no "gainful occupation" and was able to construct his own calendar, he was free to pursue a whim or dilate upon a notion with leisure more characteristic of the speculative hobo than of Boston's dutifully busy "leisure class."

While relinquishing no single privilege of the adolescent aristocrat, he made, as he grew older, more significant revolutions, which the ritual pranks but symbolized. He rebelled against the ancestral caste-religious Unitarians, becoming an Anglo-Catholic, of a never very orthodox variety. He rebelled against capitalism, becoming a member of the Socialist Labor party. An Anglican and a Socialist, he took the minority and purist and perfectionist view of each allegiance; yet in both cases he endeavored to subordinate his marked individuality to "society, the redeemed form of man."

His third rebellion was against verse merely refined and talented. He wanted a prophetic and menacing poetry. With Emerson, whom, as revolutionary and poet, he respected, he loathed the "tinkling of piano strings," would have the kingly bard "smite the chords rudely and hard." Taking the ancient and primitive view of the poet as the maker, seer, and sayer, he was impatient of less grandiose pretensions.

And Wheelwright was a poet, reared as a child on William Blake's *Songs* and in maturity never weary of arguing his theories of prosody. In 1931 he wrote his *History of the New England Poetry Club, 1915-31*, a privately printed account of a club still extant, which had Amy Lowell and Josephine Preston Peabody as rival candidates for the first presidency. After some aesthetic violence, the conservatives (under Miss Peabody) won out, despite Miss Lowell's feeling "that, were she not elected, poetic experiment would appear repudiated by her fellow New Englanders." The *History* is deliciously rich in gibes, purported naïvetés, and constant irony.

From 1928 till death, Jack was institutionally loyal to the New England Society, serving as vice-president and general minor official.

Not in accord with the refined and conventional "line" which prevailed, to the production by the lady members of rondeaux and villanelles, he attended—not to murmur appreciative sighs but to bear his witness, offer his criticism of that which had been read, as seriously as though it had been a poem by Blake or Donne.

I do take seriously the opening sentence of the *History*: "It is impossible to write poetry which is merely poetry, or American poetry which is merely American. Poetry must be poetic in a particular way; ours must be American in a New England way." Not for him the Poetry Society of America: rather than that he would put up with his fellow Bostonians, whom—difficult as they might be to take, personally or doctrinally—he regionally understood.

The "causes" which engaged him were felt to be one cause. Jack was not a dialectician; and he could not, cerebrally or verbally, have synopsized Poetry, Catholicism, and Communism; but he held, by faith, that the *summa* of the future would properly adjust their parts and demonstrate their compatibility.

In the Argument which follows his *Political Self-Portrait*, he wrote of his last book: ". . . what will emerge is rather more humanist than materialist, and much less a political treatise than a self-portrait of one who has found no way of turning, with Scientific Socialism, from a mechanical to an organic view of life than to draw from moral mythology as well as from revolutionary myth. . . . Just as the Church through Scholasticism once squared faith with reason, and just as already Christian ethics have abandoned Divine Predestination for Economic Determinism, so religion (which is the social ethic of the imagination) must transform itself and dialectic materialism." And Poetry is, of course, the mode whereby the imagination is socially operative. "The main point is not what noise poetry makes, but how it makes you think and act,—not what you make of it, but what it makes of you."

The consequence of this theory and this life was four books of poems, of which three were published in his lifetime. If most of Wheelwright's friends found it difficult to assemble him for appraisal, they found it yet more difficult to appraise his writing. They took his books as the concomitants of taking him; and taking him was—

if one cared for his ease—a high grade of intellectual excitement.

Wheelwright's published books, *Rock and Shell*, *Mirrors of Venus*, and *Political Self-Portrait*, are, to a degree almost unparalleled, extensions of his total self, private as well as professional. There are the poem-by-poem dedications to his friends, his relatives, and occasionally his favorite enemies—poems not correlated to the dedicatees save as, by principle, a man must assemble, honor, and adjust his personal and his doctrinal loyalties. Trusting the reader to "bear in mind that it is impossible to say a poem over in prose," Wheelwright felt free to supply each volume with an Argument, a copious and racy commentary upon the poems, in which he disserted (in a fashion neither Shavian nor Jamesian) upon matters bibliographical, autobiographical, ideological, and prosodic. These comments, far from prose paraphrases, should be taken before or after, not with, the poems.

There are the long "mythic" poems: "Forty Days," "North Atlantic Passage," "Twilight," "The Other." These are Wheelwright's most recalcitrant work. He has indicated their sources in the Cabala and the Talmud, the Apocryphal Gospels, "lost and hostile gospels," the Nestorian Acts of the Apostles—testimonies to his zeal for the "minority rights" even in Christian tradition. His inveterate Seth and Cain (in *Political Self-Portrait*) are, to be sure, investments of St. Augustine's *De Civitate Dei*, according to which these two sons of Adam are founders of the rival cities, mundane and spiritual, so that human history is the record of Cain's war with Seth. But even with these helps, they remain "prophetic books" in need of careful exegesis before judgment can be passed.

Mirrors of Venus, a modern *In Memoriam*, was in process of composition over a period of twenty years; and its general scheme is the poet's own movement, emotional as well as intellectual, from concern with the private self, its desire for private love and private happiness and private survival after death, to faith in the corporate solidarity of mankind, the Resurrection which is the transcendence of the "personal." But so to state it is to give the doctrine rather than the movement, which never reaches this solidarity. This too is an "Ash Wednesday." It is a flagellation of the introvert, carried out with a startling minimum of the rhetorical or elegiac; it is a determined effort to expose and castigate the sentimentalist's fine wonder at his own fine feelings.

Structurally, this effort means taking the most conventional of forms, the sonnet, the form consecrated to amatory sequences and hyperbolic compliment, and subjecting it to all manner of inversions and distortions, more radical than those of Dr. Merrill Moore. And these ingenuities—in one instance, the provision of three concurrent rhyme schemes—were intended to give writer and reader a tough, quasi-mathematical obstruction to any approach of the sentimental. In any case, it would be nearly impossible for a New Englander to have written with such central depth and candid innocence if he had not given his sequence the look of a scholastic construction. But the devices were more than protective mask: they were valiant and generally successful efforts to formalize self-pity and the like spreading and formless emotions.

The precise order in which the "sonnets" are arranged could probably be altered without disaster to the continuity, but the poems, individually ponderable, gain mass by consecutive reading, their total effect being that of a musical "suite" in which there is a general counterpoint of moods, tones, and movements. The styles are extraordinarily varied: low-pitched and conversational, or playful, or grotesque; direct or oblique; imagistic or metaphysical; thin or densely crowded; elliptical or logical. There is the conversational mode of "Sophomore," in which the sentence falls amiably into the easy verse with the unemphatic disyllabic rhyme:

> When, catching his own glance, he analyzed
> what stared so impolitely from the mirror,
> he wondered if he earnestly despised
> that callow face; or did he hold it dearer
> because, unlike his classmates, he preferred
> talk with autumnal women, ever mellow,
> or boys, with whom his well-considered word
> not always marked him as a crazy fellow?

There are the playful, didactic wit of "Mother," and the imagism of "Week End Bid I," and the *symbolism* of "Summer."

Wheelwright's obvious, difficult job was to assemble his parts; and at this he was but infrequently successful. Such integers as "Father," however, survive repeated examination.

> An East Wind asperges Boston with Lynn's sulphurous brine.
> Under the bridge of turrets my father built,—from turning sign
> of CHEVROLET, out-topping our gilt State House dome
> to burning sign of CARTER'S INK,—drip multitudes
> of checker-board shadows. Inverted turreted reflections
> sleeting over axle-grease billows, through all directions
> cross-cut parliamentary gulls, who toss like gourds.

> Speak. Speak to me again, as fresh saddle leather
> (Speak; talk again) to a hunter smells of heather.
> Come home. Wire a wire of warning without words.
> Come home and talk to me again, my first friend. Father,
> come home, dead man, who made your mind my home.

The octave and the sextet are in counterpoint: the restlessly kinetic picture of Boston from the River, not images alone but symbols of Church and State ("asperges," "parliamentary") and the Capitalism which out-tops the State; then the prevailingly monosyllabic and abruptly rhymed invocation, with its extraordinary simile, as remote as the felt distance between city scene and invoked father; the undeterred bold repetition of simple words, the sloganlike alliteration (after the fashion of an advertisement or a neon sign), the sure emphasis of the last three nouns (man, mind, home); these make a poem continuously rewarding in detail and built into a whole by the precarious mode of a two-part movement without the aid of a repetitive and conclusive third.

From these bold variations from the sonnet, Wheelwright turned to bolder experiment. Some of the poems in *Political Self-Portrait* are relics of early composition (their author was likely to keep pieces long by him, inviting and—when he assented—accepting, the aid of those to whom, so eagerly, he read them aloud); but the characteristic new work, intractable to scansion either by stress or syllable, is yet scarcely to be mistaken for pre-Eliotic free verse. In contrast to the sonnets, it offers a public poetry, to be recited or chanted unselfconsciously. Its claim to being poetry lies in its resourcefulness, its vivacity, its surprises.

Like all New Englanders, Wheelwright was a didactic poet; but he had learned some things from the mistakes of his elders: he does not carefully separate his picture from his moral or his song from his sermon; and one judges the earnestness of his propagandistic intent not by any pontifical tones but by his willingness to clown, to shout, to clatter, to repeat, to pun, to alliterate, to jingle—in order that the reader shall stop to listen and, stopping, be forced to remain alert. It was designed chiefly, I suppose, to show the "workers" that poetry need not be academic or epicene. Critically, there is no harm in calling the consequence intellectual vaudeville, if one stress the adjective equally with the noun.

Like other revolutionary poets, Wheelwright found it hard to give poetic particularity to blueprints of the Future; but he knew, with precision, what made him squirm; and he had a brilliant talent, in life and in letters, for the satire which travels from its inception in a lampoon to its finale in the caricature of a class. It is not the hatred of what he once adored: the satire bangs away at the poet's old enemies—the smug, the complacent literati, the profiteers and the frauds.

But Wheelwright's concern for a revolution—his soapbox homilies in the South End of Boston, when, raccoon-coated and elegantly waistcoated, he would, like Chekhov's "penitent noblemen," urge his listeners to do away with his Class, were never invitations to the proletariat to enjoy the delights of gadgetry. The theme of "Redemption" is a revolution which shall effect the union of Deed and Word, of Art and Christianity. In his note to the poem, he asks whether "future proletarian patronage of a public standard of sophisticated living . . . [may turn out to] be as half-hearted, almost, as present capitalist patronage?" and answers, "At any rate, one can never be premature in arousing the masses to their cultural duties and to the joy of living."

About his native city and region—for he was a regionalist whose flights to New York were brief—his feelings were equally ambivalent. "I don't hate the South," says Quentin of Mississippi to Canadian Shreve; and Jack's narratives of Boston's horrors and his indictments of the loved, confused city—vulgar and vulgarly refined—were of analogous order.

The feeling was always there: the love and devotion, the prophetic "Woe unto you"; but they reach their most subtle power in "Come Over and Help Us," a poem "written in Blake's seven beat epic meter" of the Prophetic Books, a poem which is, says Wheelwright, "a rhapsody on the type Bostonian."

The title is the "Macedonian Call" of Acts 16:19 and is "addressed to the world that is not Boston."

Our masks are gauze + and screen our faces for those unlike us only,
Who are easily deceived. + Pierce through these masks to our
                                                unhidden tongues
And watch us scold, + scold with intellectual lust; + scold
Ourselves, our foes, our friends; + Europe, America, Boston; and
                                                all that is not
Boston: + till we reach a purity, fierce as the love of God;— + Hate.
. . . .

Madness, we so politely placate + as an every-day inconvenience
We shun in secret. + Madness is sumptuous; Hate, ascetic.
. . . .
We are not tireless; + distract us from thin ecstasy, that we may hate
If with less conviction, + with some result, some end,—
So pure ourselves; so clear our passion; + *pure, clear, alone.*

The New Englander leaves New England + to flaunt his drab person
Before Latin decors + and Asiatic back-drops.
Wearies. + Returns to life,—life tried for a little while.
A poor sort of thing + (filling the stomach; emptying the bowels;
Bothering to speak to friends on the street; + filling the stomach again;
Dancing, drinking, whoring) + forms the tissue of this fabric,—
(Marriage; society; business; charity;— + *Life, and life refused.*)

The New Englander appraises sins, + finds them beyond his means,
                                                + and hoards.

Wheelwright had the New England conscience and the New England originality. There were predecessors whom he respected—Blake,

xxi

Emerson, and Emily Dickinson; but he was constitutionally incapable of imitating or being schooled, and he sounds like no one else. He had to learn for himself and say for himself, eager for the criticism of his friends, unwearying at revision, but prophetically indocile. The outcome was a poetry uneven—often, by its intensity, gritty and gnarled—but rich, inclusive; felt as well as thought; symbolized not asserted; languaged in a New England vocabulary which, like Emerson's, is both transcendental and homely.

Wheelwright was a saint; he was also a poet whose books will one day take their rightful place in American poetry and scripture.

AUSTIN WARREN

ROCK AND SHELL
POEMS 1923-1933

NORTH ATLANTIC PASSAGE

FOR HAROLD AND LEONIE STERNER

THE ARGUMENT

Man, looking at the World as form in motion, sees the enigma of the One and the Many reflected on the mirror of the past. In his desire for future security he seeks to learn from fancy and imagination the nature, if not the answer, of the enigma. But all he learns from studying the past is that facts do not fuse with truth. He learns neither the cause nor the degree of this antipathy, for the enigma clouds the mirror.

Man gives himself up to enjoying the distractions of the present show. But the paradox appears that he is part of what he sees. Dissolved into the external world, he becomes an enigma to himself. It is then that he turns towards Authority to bring him assurance.

But again fact, whether seen as Being or as Becoming, proves a foundation insufficient for the authoritative superstructure. The Reason, worn by relentless flux, fears lest it dissolve away, and leaves outer facts of sense for inner truths of thought to find Authority.

Man, shut from the outside world, is shut from the enigma. But the counter paradox appears and remains, though reason and the five senses fade: it is only upon his own internal Authority that he can accept external Authority. The soul had almost become the One, but the Many breaks through its barriers and order comes to an end. Yet Man rebels against disorder. The Reason and Memory help him only a little. But, though the senses are worn, he gathers his forces; and turned from the past, goes seeking to find that immediate and present assurance which is required.

Opal-Black, iridescent with rainbows. Rainbows
opalescent from rainbows' reflections
the while, the liquescent rainbow's crescent fades;
surface on surface,
pressed down,
weighted together, solid under the sky;
stretching undulous, like pavements lustrous
of houses of prayer, of banqueting;
black marble pavements, veined with green, creamy foam
foam fallen on spray, clustered like bullets
bullets in embryo, clust'ring round a cold bullet mould—
      Ah, leaden dragon, in those claws
        of yours you prison

flawless bubbles of crystal,
    toss them with your teeth.
You wash and crash about
    through leaden water,
    yet never smash nor flaw
    the flashing balls.

Over vulcanic waves, spray falls like wind-blown water-falls. The spray veils caves; the caves may spin with chrysoprase, in gimlets of electric light. (All good bottles are blistered in bubbles; cracked seeds of bottle-glass could be set with pearl in platinum.) From mirrored caves of radiance, scimitar cleaves scimitar, above the sandy plains which stretch below— Venusberg, Xanadu; red-bearded Rip Van Winkle's mountain; Ararat, the Assassins' mountain; the Sinai of Prometheus; Christ's!

Peace on thy hills, Jerusalem!

Across the plains, the echeloned and reinforced, salient, flank, headlong advances (stiffening hanks of molasses candy) of plagues, conquests, ravenous religions; prairie fires; out, over arid vales and ranges; out, beneath exultant fans of dominance; over, in pounding mallets of conflict.* Across, like ambushed savages; the lank shoots of,—fleeting, melting, persisting; disappearing, melted,—gone; gone the shreds of that marauding ardor,— the arcs; crescents of phosphorescence; the mallet, the scythe; swords; the sheath'd scimitar. We lift up our eyes unto the hills from whence come— sloppy waves; sloppy waves are left. Is that all? Whence but from hills comes nostalgia to fill the eyes with tears?—Let us cross the river, and rest under the shade of trees:

                This derisive dominance
                of duels, fans and common-sense;
                    this gay decadence I survey
                    diverts me, but cannot repay
                me for the gone hills, melted, gone
                    fleet to melt, yet insistent
                    resurgent falls, mountains persistent
                cascades meditated on

by sages amid rainbows; misty; as veils of chiffon cigarette smoke, progressing inward through a window; while to the croaking of three-legged toads; crippled pines fan flies from their shaved pates; and mist sifts over snowy hills; painted, yet quaking pictures trembling on paper walls shaken

---

* (Decisive Battles of the World; Influence of Sea Power upon History)

4

by hollow mountains; where, watching opal smoke drift outward, turn to mist, sit Dietrich von Bern, Hassan Sabbah; Otto Kahn and Tannhaüser,— to say nothing of King Arthur and Lord Kitchener,—

Distinct, a dolphin splashes.

Past a porpoise dashes.

One orange, two bananas, orange-red.

Unravel all mythology.

Weave a new Theosophy.

Truth lies in Correspondence, it is said.

Siva signifies thereby

Heinrich Heine's Lorelei,

Rhine salmon salted, spread on Boston Bread.

A wind like a razor shaves the lather from my whiskers. Across the floor of ashen and black marble, the hem-stitched and shirred ruching and ruffles; starched petticoats, under-and-over skirts of ball dresses, with scarves, capes, tippets, shawls, boas, and opera cloaks; all together now,—lash rush and tumble.—Flopping and swishing, frowsy, sloppy chic; sweeping swerving fan and sword dancers; Benjamin Franklin's incandescent Daughters strike attitudes of various hysteria before the zenith of Catharine the Great's umbrageous Sons. The Dance of form and light swaps with the Dance of shadow and color. In the bald-headed row, Barbarossa slumbers on the lap of Prester John,—while the budding Blossom bursts apart; its petals uncurl in acanthine grace; and the Lotus lolls serenely on the Waters.

Great God! Switch on the lights! What horns pierce through there? Ionic horns, tin goat horns, the Dragon's horns! You crustaceous reptile, who are not unlike a spider; who are very like a larch tree; you hemlock with fanged boughs. You savage Worm, who am I am that I am; who am I that I am that I am you?

The Enemy, bite it! Bleeding gobbets, in your maw, congeal to tusks and talons. Your scales are its frighted foam; yet, drop willing it not; a dancer driven mad; from a flight of pheasants to a dog a-crawl on all fours, Protean monster,—sunk but once, you dissolve (as I melt before you) to what you most detest, being most yourself.—

Christians, to please the Mother of God

call her the Star of the Sea.

Some bores shake their troubled heads

because waves squander solar energy.

More sigh, "Beauteous!" when they glimpse

merfolk, at their wayward play.

5

Celestials, in claws and scales of spray
perceive the teeth, the scales, the claws
of the Dragon of Time, in the Abysm.
Excellent embodiments of Philosophy,
four compendiums of Wisdom.

O Virgin, from whom Earth stole her name of Mother; deep tank of our
own Blood; Mammal of Birth; thou Cistern how profound; whale very like
a camel; camel in the needle's eye; mirror of the eye of God; vanity-case of
the Moon; O terrible Cradle which is Woman's hair! Womb of waters, into
which the Spirit of water breathed. (Foamy birth of Venus) Tomb of waters,
into which the Son of God swam. (undrainable flagon of Thor) Loom of
waters whereon Form is manifest of wandering Nautilus of pilgrims'
scallop-shell; and of more stately mansions, O my Soul! Composite acan-
thus, capturing Ionic volutes; crowned with the opening Lotus; ready to
receive the Compassionate Lord of Peace; ready, but shattered; demolished
too soon to receive the Rapture.

Scalloped whitecaps; with their spuming
flakes, as light as Autumn ashes;
climbing never, always mounting
slipping always, never sinking
under a kinetic torrent
manufacture, close at hand
in the wake (a Tyrol current
clear, against its distant bank)
peacock-eye-like, ostrich-plumey
classic frets, Chinese lattices.

First-begotten of the First-begotten; Live space; Fragrance of Purity;
Marriage Bed of Force and Form; Succubus of Death; Charnel of Birth;
Cesspool of Stinkage,—where exhausted or unfulfilled shapes: of fan coral,
of trailing anemone, shape of the polypus, octopus, floundering devil-fish;
squid; shape of the dashing porpoise, and the flashing dolphin: spread out,
mingle together, squirm to be distinct; where slops from cities issue, and
dishwater from farms; banana, orange-peel and toilet paper at one with the
Fulfillment & Source of All; into which course at length foeti, dropped
in the mud of the street, or flung from a ruddy window.

Behold!
all in the midst
the floating point
diminishes, to the noise of conches

6

and kettle-drums, tabors and drums and cowhorns.

Lo, it is he, the Tortoise.

The Circle, which is a Polygon.

Inscribe a circle on air.

That can never not have been accomplished.

Such is he.

Neither does he change his Position amid Positionless Change.

Before him, this tumult flattens to pewter.

Does the Calm blind thee? Thou hast misused thine eyes.

See only He.

Force not the shapes about thee to thy form.

Call not the Ocean, Mother.

Give no one thy Name; no one; not he.

While thou art determined to wed with the Flood

(Remember, be comforted)

It is more than unthinkable for him to deviate from his nature.

He is the Tortoise; he is not the Lotus.

Should the Hexagon unfold!

Behold!

As we melt before him

the Blossom, amid whose Perfume

Water is Ice and Steam.

The Turtle bursts not, but pulls its six limbs in,—head, legs and tail. I listen to a gong, distinct from centers which surround It, sounding down my ears to silence chaos:

"'Tis he who melts, not thou."

Beneath the circumference, peripheral dissonance deafens me; leading my hearing out; beyond my ultimate perimeter; to the encircling center—Indistinct—Smell the odours of Incubi and the wounds of the World. The Eyes is upon us ever since the Begotten of Wisdom descended down deep through the watery tomb.

To the hills for your lives!

The dam has burst!

Terrible, oh, terrible! God's vanity is bloody. (Womb ript; Loom broke.) Give the natural products and chief industries of the Land of Lyonnesse. Name him who stole the Earth away. (Big Double Bed consumed by flames. Pound tin dish pans, wave your torn banners.) Although Whales and Seals remain mammals amid waters, you, if you are virginal, detest most what you melt to, and the dog whose manger you crawl into,

Let us go a-hunting pheasants of Flight—
Ah, remould the bullets from their clustered spray on fallen foam.
—Put out the lights, in the houses of lustrous ceilings,
undulous outstretched sky—
Send forth a word, that the world be flooded with silence.
We must find the needle in the Camel's Haystack
so put out the light.
—Lead us on there, by deadened surfaces
over faded, imitation marble
past our incessant reflection, in cracked mirrors
under dusky, wax-dripping chandeliers
dustily swaying, to and fro
a-glow with crescent, broken crystal.

> Lead us from opalescent
> rainbows, through rainbows
> to black opal—

THE INCEPTION OF THE CROSS

FOR ROBERT HILLYER

After the Fall
of Lucifer
Michaël
who battled well
healed clean
by Raphaël
leans
in the highest sphere
heavily
on his spear.

All
as before:
Dominion
Throne
touching pinion

8

tip to tip
zone
infinity.

But radiant choristers
and windy thurifers
groan
and roar
before
Trinity.

Out from whose midst drums
the sound of the Name
on whose breath
from an egg of flame
one comes

far
piercing the deep dark
whence fell
the Day-Star
the black that gapes
close at the son's place
spattered with grapes:
Satan's space.

Heaven weeps.
The ellipse
of Hell is full
of cool tears
till
the Ineffable
cries:

"Open your eyes.
See
Wailing ones
he
is beautiful;

he is an archangel,—
the cross, skull-shod.
Death is the cross of winged moons
where hangs God."

SLOW CURTAIN

FOR MARY OPDYCKE PELTZ

Two lovers face one another
actor and actress
   author and conjoint authoress
   manager, promptress
   property man and make-up woman.
It is an amateur performance
   but the piece is well written
   but the lines imply the business
   but the piece means little
   but the last two words read:
   They kiss.
The actors are their own audience.
   As actors, they are artists.
   As audience, they are critics.
   They have read the play beforehand
   in order to do it justice,
   and they know the final stage directions
   are impossible.
The piece comes to an end.
   The lovers face one another.
   Neither moves a muscle.
There is no applause.

QUICK CURTAIN

FOR MARY OPDYCKE PELTZ

All the while, within the chamber
camera men awaited our embrace
  which never came.
Our hearts like clocks beat near
near, nearer, and more near
  with every footfall up the corridor.
There was yet time to be alone.
(Never before had we known the generosity of seconds)
There was yet time,
and in that time, our lifetime.
All the pictures floated forward from the wall
  upward, and to the right;
  —no—upon looking again,
  downward, and to the left.
She heard the me of years-to-come speak loud:
  "I never write you;
  I hardly ever think of you;
  Yet what I think and do
  is thought and done
  with reference to you."
Operators behind the ceiling
had tangled up the wires
and taut cords held our heads high.
  I could not turn a quarter-circle
  nor advance the requisite half-step
  to lift my arms up, move them over
  and drop my head on hers
  with the abrupt simplicity of a doll.
  Light pierced the leaves and flecked the mirrors;
  clear and clearer, and more clear
  the sun swam through the lessening rain.
  We had grown wise in all things before love.

SEED PODS

FOR LOUISE DAMON

Where the small heads of violets
are shrunk to smaller skulls,
in meadows where the mind forgets
its bull fights and its bulls;
the dust of violet or rose
relinquishes its scent
and carries with it where it blows
a lessening remnant
of heresies in equipoise
and balanced argument
with which the mind would have refleshed
the flower's skeleton,
but that it found itself enmeshed
in the web of oblivion.
Therefore, when Gabriel sound the horn
and dust rise through the ground,
our flesh shall turn, on our last morn
fleshless as the horn's sound.

FORTY DAYS

FOR CHARLES HENRY COSTER

THE ARGUMENT

I

The risen Christ came to show not questioning but doubt to the Apostles as the arena of Faith. They, knowing neither His form nor speech, judged Him as the Church judges many Saints. Under this trial He was proved an Heresiarch and brought curses on His head, which He answered with impossible commands, and a terrible revelation.

II

The doubting Apostle who tells of this strays through his memories—the recognition of Peter; the acts of Jesus after His triumphal entry into Jerusalem; His teaching to the disciples of the Baptist by Jordan River; the dark night after his death; the gathering news of His rising again; His morning greeting to James.

III

The Apostle proceeds to tell how Christ, after prophesying the manner of His departure and last coming, mounted into the sky a second time transfigured. The Eleven, when they saw Him go, fell into an ecstasy; but called back to things as they are, each carried his own death with him to the center of men's will,—that is to say, the city of God on earth.

I

a. The sun at his zenith
hangs, directly overhead to all men.
So, to each of us, face to face, directly;
Jesus stood,—
cooling his wounded feet
in the surface clay of the pasture,
watching goat-men drive their goats
from right to left, below the mound
along a road with sudden bends
to shear them in the cave where he was born.

q. *While goat-men sheared their herd*
in the cave past our left hand
What was his final word?

Will you comprehend?
—"Say it not," we cried
"Say not 'I am that I am' or we kill you.
We want to know where the Lord is."
And we all ran together, closing the circle.
Like swords, our threats turned in our throats.
"Say not 'I am I' lest we make you nought
and we would only ask you to lead us where we would go"
and he came on inward, and
He,
the center,
was gone.

p. *What had he said? Can I remember?*
"Fools of God, wise in loud words
I am not truth, I am He."

o. *And before that had said*: "Judge not
though I would tip the scales
of all who weigh
and, at each tilt, exact
more silver for less gold."

n. *And before* "Judge to precipitate contagious act.
Judge not the act
which gives the power to judge.
Ask not for *Why*. Ask only for the *How*.
Judge not two words I bring you,
Yes and *No*; these two shall not taste death.
All other words take meanings I make strange."

m. *And before that had said:*
—"Lies trap the doors of mouth and ears,
at the tongues and teeth of questioning
where thought falls, prone.
There I listen with the ears of a liar,
but watch for thought, whether *Yes* or *No*,
poised in silence for them who keep silence."

l. *While blue flax dropped its petals before noon;*
the goats were herded to the cave.
—"Ask and receive," he said.
"Speak, be silent, reject, do not question.
Be not as dogs guarding lambs

14

but weak as only the strong dare seem:
be sheep in the midst of wolves."
—"What, mocking shepherd, if the lambs be killed?"
"Lambs never fear wolves after death."

k. *What had he said while, through still heat*
blue flowers slept in private nights?
"My second birth makes you unborn to me,
sheep, heard through fog.
(See the flax close before the mounting sun)"
Do I remember the wonder?
"Strugglers, your dark questioned leapings
wedged embers between rock
in a certain place, towards the left hand
whence now their pent light
I loose from caves, reborn."

j. *Lizards sought creviced refuges from heat*
Can I remember what he said?
—"Go on searching till you find.
When you have found, you wonder.
He that wonders, does well
and in working takes his rest."

i. *Below the mound the goat-men called*
their herds to halt.
While drooping flax flowers bowed
John, who was wise among us, cried:
—"What is truth? By your words
there is but little in the world."
And he replied:
—"They in the world measure their truth.
Know their measures, and know my truth."
—"Rumor speaks a wiser answer
of Jesus,—who kept silent."
—"I have not come here now
to act out wisdom among
the wise in desire for knowledge
and the unwise not to discern,
but for you to seek to know form
as the blind know, who see not light nor shade."

h. *I remember now*

15

how turning full on Peter, he replied:
"Do we cheat your eyes who need
no shade to show our form?
Give me one to know our dark roots of doubt.
He will need light to see our pods of truth
no more than I need shade to be made seen."

g. *What was said before that?*
Do I remember how Peter had answered?
"You cheat
who tip our measured scales that weigh!
You do not seek truth.
Neither is it truth we seek.
We seek the One in the Maze.
You are the Devil.
You are a devil who *this,*—
a bodiless demon who *that,*—
you are a devil who:—
furthermore; why do you cast no shadow?"

f. *He said, while lizards crept*
forth to the morning heat:
"The golden bars are not your own
nor silver coin
only your scales are yours,
so test these scales.
Empty both pans to hold the level dial
and watch the tongue tilt swift, and soon less swift,
tilt back, to near its pause, pass its true crisis
repass, and stand still. Look how the tongue has bent
since it was given you, Peter.
Whose gold could tell the white coins' weight
with your scales' twisted tongue?"

e. *What had he said before?*
Do I remember?
—"Lay hold on me, handle me. Try me in your scales.
But test the scales with first and greater care.
True scales and false all come to balance.
No man can judge scales until they be emptied.
You are a judge, indeed,
but your judged one reverses your judgment."

16

d. *While sunbeams tickled sluggish lizards*
   to the wise stranger, we,
   strangers to wisdom, replied:
   —"You do not ask us what we give.
   Word-changers long ago, now we are judges.
   Why would you have us unmask words?
   We will not, for your prongs of doubt
   snatch truth from men who handle thought.
   We do not test words. As Judges we weigh souls
   to prove from scales once given us,
   if any judge preside within."

c. *To what did we make answer*
   while the last morning dew upon the meadows dried?
   Lip to ear, and ear to mouth
   a score of ears, two lips, one tongue
   had said:—"Be money changers. Retain
   good metal, reject bad. Ye Exchangers,
   in you, God weighs his scales.
   Free from all dangers, prove my words
   even as you proved silver."

b. *So much do I remember. Dust of goats*
   rose on the distant right, and near words fell:
   —"Grasp me between your fingers.
   Break me in twain.
   Suck the honey unprisoned
   from the bee's cracked belly.
   Suck bees' honey.
   Fear not the sweetness.
   Rather fear (it is a brave fear)
   something foreign to the sweet
   some bitter sap, memorial brine
   which sours passion too much lingered on.
   Thomas, remember my sting.
   It is not questioning, but doubt."
   So much do I remember.
   I remember all but the wonder.

II

Those days before we grew half-used
  to breathing air suffused
  with presences to tend our want;
the days when we had only thought him . . .
  thought him only a more imperious Rabbi,
  Rabbi, who had entered
  to expiate the sin of Abel;
imperious Prophet, who had quenched
  the fire on the bloody Altar;
Prophet, who dared to have entered the Holy of Holies
  seeking the Key of Knowledge hidden there
  by them who go not in themselves
  and open not to them who would go in—
  searching for his Kingdom's Key
  the Key to his Kingdom
  to which he is Doorway and Door
  and when he had found it, had given it Peter.
Hid Elohim, till the Secret
  gushing from Peter's mouth
  made our tongues prick
  and the nape of my neck
  tingle, as with sprinkled water.
Elohim, before the Dove descended
  bearing in her beak a twig
  dripping from the tree of life
  fluttering above him,
  dropping the sap on him
  making him christ
  with the living chrism;
who, while moist from the river bathing,
  yet thirsted for despair;
  and said to them who grew weak with their fastings:
  —"Not one of you hungers.
  You weaken me with your weakness
  who listen only with the inward ear
  and miss me seeing with one eye.
  It is for the hungry I hunger.

I have found others filled and drunken
and now I find you emptied of all thirst.
Fast not; and eat of every herb
but of that herb bitter in itself
eat not—
Your hands, then, will not reach
to the middle of the world
nor your gods, then, forsake you."

In the sarcastic stillness of catastrophe
shame numbed us.
I sat all day with no food
turning with blueing, unrecording eyes
his scroll of Enoch
thinking him sinless, *if folly be not sin.*

★ ★ ★

The news of his rising at first seemed natural;
(like daybreak after the gray doubt)
and much less lonely so.
We woke to live when his brother came,
James the austere, the just,
told, ran and told;
came running to say:
that the Lord no sooner had given his grave-cloth
to Malchus in the High Priest's House
than the Lord was before James where he lodged,
asking for a table and bread—
took the bread, brake, and commanded:

—"Eat, brother; forget to fast
and in forgetting, forget them who hunger.
Know what you are doing, and be saved;
know not, and be with all who go against my Law.
But knowing or unknowing
take my bread and eat—
a sleeper wakens with me, from among the sleepers."

III

—Forty days
and forty nights, which were as days
starlight, moonlight, lamplight, sunlight
fell on his form, compact of light,
as, on dark form shade falls.
To feel him with us was enough
enough to have a look in flashing moments
how his neck behind his ear
sloped to the beam-like shoulder of the Carpenter.
He was made visible
by no shadow, shade, nor any modeling;
only the bright body of his body's light
made dark all light I knew.
O! whirring feathers, darting Dove,
that dripping twig
those drops of chrism, and—
the Christ!

—The fortieth day was spent.
He took a wild black iris between his toes
plucked it, and let it fall.
(I thought even him reluctant to give up
friendships he had found sweetly
bedded in life's bitterness.)
—"I go!
Going, I precede you.
I come
and coming, judge you by those things
in which I precede you.
Nor shall I come again till two be one:
till top be bottom; left be right;
all that which is without, within;
male with the female, each both male and female:
future and forward, past and left behind."
And speaking, grew less tangible
than to the three on the transfigured mount.
"I have shown you my glory.

As a bee leaves the flower
I go,
but cleave a seed—I am there;
split the rock, you shall find me,
and where the lonely ones
gather together, there I am."

I saw him stretch his arms,
I thought him tired and yawning,
but, with a shock of shame, I knew
the benediction in the attitude.
(I had not seen him die.)
We saw his wounds glow red,
the body fulminate
and Him of Fire,
mounting on subservient Seraphim
whirl, twist away.

The arms had stretched as if for flight—
the five Scars glowed—
his chest lifted as for breath,
and his heels, as if for dancing;
between, beneath his toes
the red clay clung and kissed them.—
The legs hung from the hips
a bell below the torse,
swung like a bell below the hips;
he lifted his chin in song.
The smoking robe consumed in flame:
White flames, Petals of Lilies
Lilies of Flame, Dimmed by the effulgence of the Flesh.
There, a triumphal statue with no pedestal, he stood;
then mounted higher on the air.
The footprints ringed wider
like footprints on still water
ringed, broke into stars, wings, legionary eyes.
In rushing flight about him
in spheres and disks, the Seraphim
Span, Whirled, Twisted

Flickered, Gleamed away.
Away, toward the opened Firmament
through the triangular Name above it.
Above It,
away.

—We gaped and shook our heads and gazed
after what had passed before our eyes.
He.
Not a cynic, no blasphemer
No Rabbi; not a daemon
not a devil, and no Prophet.
He.
The One, the True God, going to his Father in Heaven
as to his Mother on Earth, he came, the One, the True
the Lord.
We stared not only in wonder, not with loneliness,
feeling him with us, permanent . . .

"Gluttonous bees! Come forth."
—Two Strangers sudden beside us
standing in the midst of praise.
"Forth, gluttonous bees!
Swarm!
Come from the blossomed eye
the germ of act, the seed to split the rock
forth; come forth; swarm."

We turned and fled; not as we had fled
from that disturbed suburban orchard
not so now, we were fleeing
toward the City, not away from it.
Our heads were buffeted by Clubs, by Stones
Swords, Glaives, Knives, Saws, Spears, bit our feet.
Our blood spattered our paths.
Forward, Sideward, Backward, Forward
four pitched prone;
lay, like fallen crucifixions
a moment, then on again.

I, and the other Son of Thunder
plunged down hill
with backs bowed, with eager brows
like angelic Centaurs we saw riding
Above, Behind, Below, Before, About us
whom, Within us and Without us,
we heard shouting:
—"Rome!
to Rome,
Rome!
Go to Rome!
Go tell the Roman Synagogue.
Tell Rome!"

WHY MUST YOU KNOW?

FOR ETHEL RIPLEY THAYER

—"What was that sound we heard
fall on the snow?"
  —"It was a frozen bird.
Why must you know?
All the dull earth knows the good
that the air, with claws and wings
tears to the scattered questionings
which burn in fires of our blood."
—"Let the air's beak and claws
  carry my deeds
far, where no springtime thaws
  the frost for their seeds."
—"One could fathom every sound
that the circling blood can tell
who heard the diurnal syllable,
while lying close against the ground."
—"My flesh, bone and sinew
  now would discern
hidden waters in you
  Earth, waters that burn."

23

—"One who turns to earth again
finds solace in its weight; and deep
hears the blood forever keep
the silence between drops of rain."

WOULD YOU THINK?

FOR ETHEL RIPLEY THAYER

Does the sound or the silence make
music? When no ripples pass
over watery trees; like painted glass
lying beneath a quiet lake;
   would you think the real forest lay
   only in the reflected
   trees, which are protected
   by non-existence from the air of day?
Our blood gives voice to earth and shell,
they speak but in refracted sounds.
The silence of the dead resounds,
but what they say we cannot tell.
   Only echoes of what they taught
   are heard by living ears.
   The tongue tells what it hears
   and drowns the silence which the dead besought.
The questioning, circumambient light
the answering, luminiferous doubt
listen, and whisper it about
until the mocking stars turn bright.
   Tardy flowers have bloomed long
   but they have long been dead.
   Now on the ice, like lead
   hailstones drop loud, with a rattlesnake's song.

ANY FRIEND TO ANY FRIEND

$$(A-B)^2 = (B-A)^2$$

FOR BERNARD BANDLER

On outskirts of the woods of thought
  B saw *A* bow his head
to mourn the death of one *B* sought . . .
  and found himself was dead.

A dug one grave for corpse and man.
  And turned aside to laugh.
But when *B* rose to dig, *A* ran
  upon *B* with the staff,

which *B* had cut *A* when it leaved
  (though it ran blood, not sap)
There was no combat. They both grieved,
  fallen, across the dead man's lap.

MOSSY MARBLES

FOR HESTER CHANLER PICKMAN

Marble lyres mark
  Where minor singers slumber,
And glistering night weeps
On willows above their graves;
But a wordless wind sweeps
  Over the solid dark
As over Sappho's waves
  Of keen thinkers without number.
The weakling who has known
  A small grief has his meekness.
They who can teach and show
  Know words he never names
Who sweeps the sobbing bow,
  Whom Pity quickly claims.

Pity the strong alone
   Who seldom show their weakness,
Whose hearts break with no sign
   But withered lips and tresses,
Who know, if sounding chord
   To all their thought were given,
If they trod out the wine
   Longed for, from memory's presses,—
The dissonances, poured
   Would sour their own heaven.

TWILIGHT

A PARAPHRASE

FOR SAMUEL FOSTER DAMON

Those golden skeins, those clean as the sea,
those of linen, those hyacinthine,
or like red lightning, and the purpureal
stood for the six allotted lands
where, now, after twelve years, we twelve go.
Two skeins fell to only one man.
Their color is not remembered,
their meaning was unpleasing.
Even when each was split
the dye was seen throughout
to be of the Indies.

If one must go through India,
which stretches from the Ocean to the Darkness,
one goes disguised;—
if one must go to India
unwilling, doubtful, and fearful;
still feeling one's fingers
probe the loved Wound;—
if one must go towards India
one goes by sea.
I have sailed fast on a fair wind.

—Climb up out of the boat, Thomas,
under the evening star.
 Go straight through the twin
stone masts of the water-gate.
—Push against this voice of flute players
water-organs and trumpets.
—Today has been a holiday in our town.
—The gods of our town sent you.
—Give your good will to the marriage we herald
of our King's daughter.

*The twelve Apostles cast
lots for their journeys to
the six ends of the earth.*

*Judas, called Thomas
(that is to say, the Twin)
knew the historians and
geographers taught how
India was divided into
three parts. The first was
said to end in Ethiopia,
the second at Media, and
the third to complete the
country. He was reluctant
to accept his lot. But
the Lord made Thomas
go; and after adventures
not told here, he set out
on a coasting vessel which
put in at a port on the
way.*

27

When they pass the perfume round
dip a little ointment from the jar—so—
for the eyebrows, ears, nostrils, and mouth.
Neglect not the tongue,
and rub your heart well.
Now, as the myrtle garlands are strawed
and the revellers crown one another,
wreathe from a spray of oak leaves
a crown for your own head.
But for your sceptre, choose a reed
now, as the floors are strewn.

*Though I lie down with these people
who lie down to feast,
I drink nothing, I feel unable to eat
at this wedding. The wine tastes to me
as though I had changed it to water.*

The flute girl holds the flute in her hands
as she goes among the couches.
She is of my people
and sees me, and sounds her reed
over my head a long, long time.
Should I raise my eyes, our eyes
would fly forth like birds, and birds mating.
Also the cupbearer knows me.
(He was in Jerusalem on my day of fear)
He passes me the cup;
our eyes know one another.
He has struck me across the face!
"Your act may be forgiven you in death,
but I shall have that hand
brought to me by a dog."

*The mock sceptre broke.
The myrtle of the crown
dug down into my head, like thorns.*

The curtains move.
Our eyes turn to the stairs
which lead to the higher tables.

The curtains part. The bride
stands before the revellers.

"Thou maid and child of light
to see thee is to look, steadfast, on majesty.
Thy skirts, like spring flowers
give forth a good, green smell.
Thy forehead is carved with the King, seated
feeding those seated beside him.
Truths rest from their labors
reposing behind thine eyes;
with thy feet, little joys are shown forth plain.
Thy teeth sing thee praise;
and thine hands answer each to each
like the dancing chorus of ages.
Thy fingers are keys to the gate of a tower.
Thy tongue is a curtain behind a door
drawn for him whoever enters.
Thy neck rises like the stair
whereon man mounts to learning.
Thy chamber, when warm, breathes balsam and myrrh.
It is bowered with iris and myrtle,
and carpeted with vernal laurel, and oak leaves.
About thee, stands a wall of seven men—
groomsmen of thy choosing.
Seven girls dance before thee,
while Twelve spy out the desires of thy lover.
They shall all lie down to share his lasting joy.
They shall all fall away out of time.
They shall all sink deep away into happy light;
for they have eaten food which takes away desire
and drunken wine which takes all thirst away.
They are the Sons of knowledge,
They are the Daughters of wisdom."

—The song of the stranger dies
which could not outlive our silence.
—And now it is for us as though
we had not heard one sound.

*But he was too far from
her to have her hear him;
and of those close by, only
the Flute girl heard his
pathos.*

29

—Only the flute girl continues to hear it
but then, she is of his blood.
—Even she stands off from him
and plays her flute to us; and to us alone.
(Yet she looks at him more and more
for he grows ever beautiful under her eyes.)
—The flute girl's tune wanes at the close
as though it died in love.
—She lies down before him,
and gazes and gazes upon him.
(But he looks down at the ground,
waiting until he can go.)
—(The cupbearer moves to the fountain
to cool his smarting hand.)

—I heard thunder!
—There is no wrath in the sky.
—(A royal lion breaks from his cage.
He scorns the flesh of what he kills and rends.
—One black dog seizes a hand.
—It runs up into the feast
wagging its tail, whining with pride.
—The dog has dropped the cupbearer's hand
between the stranger's feet.)

—O King! Come down to our feast! Tell
what is this man we have taken in among us?
—(The King descends; the flute girl
snaps her pipe, and throws the halves away.)

—Rise, who command my lions!
Come back, come up with me.
You, whom even my dogs revenge,
bless my daughter.

—He has already given one blessing,
—And, though we did not talk to one another,
and were still,
it is as though we had not heard one word.

Christ! Could I have made them hear?

30

For, though I watched,
I have not seen you at this feast.

—Rise! I command you
Thomas! who have command
over my lions and whom my guests cannot hear,
come, my daughter will hear you—
give her a blessing.
If one must go towards a strange marriage bed
one goes with a blessing,
but one goes unwilling, doubtful, and fearful, nevertheless.

—Rise! I command you, Thomas,
command your own reluctance
who command our desires.
I send all but the bridegroom
forth from the presence of my daughter.
Come, give her your blessing.

What shall you say to the lovers
they have not said already?
What is there, left over to say?
I am in a strange land:

"O my Lord, who go with me always
leading me, when I trust You,
uncovering the hid
and speaking the unspoken;
who planted the good tree
and taught it to bear fruit.
You, in ever-labouring change
ever the same, ever at rest,
You are in all, and are to come in all,
our courage of life, who overcome the foe,
before whom all doors open
and behind whom all mount the wide sky—
I pray You now, who at another marriage
did mix water with water, so that both ran wine,
as at Your first miracle, so now at this espousal
as body with body merges, espouse the good and the happy."

Thomas, again reluctant,
pondered as he went how
to cast the burden of his
duty on God's shoulders.

31

* * *

Beware! Beware!
It is to come
saying in your hearts
"I am the Christ."
Do not believe.
Reserve your faith. Be proud.
Be stubborn. Be hard.
What is sinful in man before God
is virtuous before this one;
believe, or obey—
your obedience and belief
compound your damnation.

Lo! these are Its marvels
told by the groomsmen:
That ye may know It and not be deceived:
It will say to the Sun
"Be dark." And the Sun darkens.
It says to the darkness, "Shine."
And the black sun shall be brilliant.
It will turn the moon to blood,
and make it bleed away;
It will walk rivers of blood
over seas as on dry land.
It will make the lame walk after It;
the deaf shall hear It; the blind see It;
It and the dumb talk long together.
Its hands shall make lepers be thought clean
and Its spittle, cause the sick
to act as though they were whole.
It will cast out devils
that the world may be cast to devils.
It heals diseases
that minds may be diseased.
It will do all that Christ does, but
It shall raise no one from death—

32

Lo! These are Its earmarks
shown by the bridesmaids:
That ye may know It and not be deceived:
It is weakly, and young, and lame,
there are bald, white places on Its temples.
Look at Its hands!
Those scabs are not scars.
Study It not in your heart
consider It not in your eyes,
lest It alter Itself to accord with your will
and shift Its behavior
to insinuate into your sense.
But, though Its whole head flame before your nerves,
you can tell It always, for
It cannot change Its hands.
Lo! The King, your father, sends us from your chamber
Yet, while we go, we leave warning behind:
This one comes in the form of Christ.
We Watchers listen for another's coming.

    Christ, when He comes
    comes in the form of a Dove
    ringed with Doves around,
    and a Sign before;
    seven rings of seven Doves
    hovering from Heaven,
    the Cross, which is a Voice,
    shining from the East to the West.

★ ★ ★

—(Tread lightly, we must tread lightly;
it is not yet dawn.
Let your foot-falls sound no louder,
no louder
than the cries on the wind
of sailors, who are putting a boat,
by the water-gate
this early, off from the quay.
—The lovers still lie sleeping.

*In the morning the Ruler
and his Consort entered
with their Servants to the
chamber of the Loved One
whose Servants they had
sent away.*

33

But spread the table for breakfast
and bring it before the bridegroom,
the bridegroom and the bride.)

—What is come over you, our children?
Why do you sit opposite each other
like an old man and wife?

—O my mother and my father,
my knowing, aged father,
law-givers in all things:
After you sent the seven
groomsmen from my bedroom
all went forth; the door shut,
and my husband raised the canopy.
Then someone came through the door
(though the door did not open before him)
who laid himself on the bed
and motioned us apart to sit on chairs.

His kindly eyes reproved us.
And what he then said is now repeated round me
as, behind these mirrors
all which has passed before their surfaces
might be repeated.
"Keep in mind, my children
what the Apostle said;
and to whom he entrusted your love
—the Everlasting Arms.
And this know—that if you refuse this thing
you become double Temples
to Virtue unweakened by Act."
—I was told it was not a bad act, I said.
It is the seed of children,
as my mother told me.
"The child destroys the parent.
Beget one child, and you beget many Sins.
For its sake, you will tell yourselves
(though, truly, it will be for your own Pride)
you envy widows and rob orphans.

34

(Your Sin will hurt others; it will hurt you more.)
Beget many children, and you beget many Ills;
of many children,
some are bound to be moon-struck, some half-witted;
some unable to walk;
some not to hear, some not to speak;
or unable to see.
Even if all be wholesome,
some will be good-for-nothing—shiftless, perverse;
some will be adulterers, murderers, thieves, or bestial;
some secretly—some even openly;—
and you—struck down in the sight of all.
Mine are the pitying Hands
which shield your backs from the Flail,
and catch you up from Life,
and wipe away your Tears,
Touch not this unclean Thing—
Pain will not touch you.
You will never be cast down.
You shall bear invisible Children
who shall ever look to the Marriage
of virgin Truth, undefiled by Thought.
You and these Children—
Mankind, and all Mankind's Ideals
shall enter to the Bridegroom's Bed!"
—When we heard this, we believed
and sat here on our chairs all night.

—Children! You show us sorrow
at the hour when we looked to joy.
Do you not love one another?

—I love my wife with pure love!

—I love my husband greatly.
I shall always be in love;
and always hold my husband to my love.

—Is it for that purpose, daughter,
that you now sit naked before him?

—The mirror of shame is clouded before me, mother;
never again can my body abash my husband.
I am subject neither to pleasure nor to passion
since neither pleasure nor passion is to be found in me.
My mind is free from lewdness and bitterness of heart;
I am cheerful—very cheerful, and I am happy;
I shall go down to the grave able to say
"I have always been very happy."

—Speak up, man, tell her
she will go to her grave a fool.

—I hold this husband of mine as of no account, father.
I have lost all memory of my marriage to this lover.
I have joined myself in a marriage which is *different*,
to another, *different*, husband—my soul's twin.

—Are you turned entirely to a woman, my young man
that you answer our daughter while she speaks,
and continue, though she continue,
with your voice rising shriller and shriller?

—Thanks to the Lord
shown forth in Me
I am freed of disease
and healed of the wound
slow to heal
cleansed of the illness
hard to make well—
called love!
Earthy manure lifts away
from before young shoots of lively seed.
God shows himself to Me
as though in mirrors where
I looked to see Me stand!

—True gods, my son, are to be seen
not in ourselves, but in other men.
This is the law whereunder the Eternal
incarnates itself in Time.

36

—From blinding Time, I set Me free, I say.
I see. I did not fall
I brought Me back and lead Me
from falling, to Higher Places.
I rise. I join Me with Me.
I search out what I was
and what I am, that I again
be what I was before.
I was not I, until I showed Me to Me
in love that flameth so, it burneth all I say.
All I tell of Love
is only a little Song.
Love findeth no fault in Me
that I cannot think hard Thoughts.
for Love loveth little Thoughts,
as Love loveth little children—
and it is Love, it is Love that singeth
My little Love Song.

—Go out quick round the town,
get me that man whom I led with mine own hand
into mine house to bless mine only daughter.
When you have him, tear him in two
as I tear my robe.
But first, flay his skin from him
and rub in vinegar, with salt.
See that you rend him before these children,
whom he sundered.

—The Jew has left town.
—A sail just passed the farthest harbor.
—We sought him high and low,
but found only the flute girl, patting the dog
and gazing where the morning star had faded.
—She is weeping.

With this miscarriage of the Gospel the Apostle left port and continued whither he had been sent.

PAUL AND VIRGINIA

FOR MY BROTHER'S CHILDREN

Nephews and Nieces,—love your leaden statues.
Call them by name; call him "Paul." She is "Virginia."
He leans on his spade. Virginia fondles a leaden
fledgling in its nest. Paul fondles with his Eyes.
You need no cast in words. You know the Statues,
but not their Lawns; nor words to plant again
the shade trees, felled; ponds, filled, and built over.
Your Garden is destroyed, but there are other Gardens
yet to spare from the destroying Spoor
unseen, save in destructful Acts. Unseen
a hungered Octopus crawls under ground
as Fungus; eats the air as Orchids on all trees;
and on all waters spreads translucent Slime.
Nephews and Nieces, who would breathe sweet Air
and till rich Ground, spy out against its suction;
wither these spreading tentacles, these roots
and radicles of cancerous Greed.

Let us put Paul and Virginia back in the Garden's
warmth of wet Box and Arbor Vitae. The Bell-Tree
a silver shrub from Japan, is grown up Big
like a willow whose Branches nose the Ground. They root
and eat the Earth. They drink deep water springs
while finger twigs fill neighboring winds with silent
tinkles of Petals, blowing on Lilies-of-the-Valley
on Larches, on copper Beeches, urn-like Elms
on Lilies, Iris, Roses walled with Hedges
mirrored on dark waters and, light with fruit trees,
on Peonies abiding in quiet pomp with leaden
Statues in a Garden, alive with Bugs and Toads.
This Garden, sad as a ripe joy is sad (dead Garden)
sheds no perfume of Soil, over a soil-less land.
This dead Garden's seeds take root in children
like the Cherry a young girl swallowed,—Stem,

Meat, and Stone; to bud, to bloom, to fruit
and to house twittering Birds.

In your Mother and Father, much you love is memory;
and much they love in you is memory transplanted
from Gardens of Love, which speak to Love from a dead
world to another, and from Death, which speaks to life
through love remembered. Nephews and Nieces,—love
your Statues, love their names.

PLANTATION DROUTH

FOR BENJAMIN RUFUS KITTREDGE, JR.

It has not rained.
The fields lie powdered
under smoke and clouds.
The swamps are peopled
with smouldering cedar
reflected on black, hoarded water.
The furrow in the field
behind the negro's heels
smokes, as though the plowshare stirred
embers in the earth.
As the furrow lengthens;
the rising powder fades to sky-dust
below the powdered sky.
This spongy land is parched
and draws the salt sea to it,
up all its earthy rivers.
It drinks brine, like a thirsty goat.
The river reeds are withered.
It is April in the meadows
but, in the empty rice fields
it is Winter.
The roots of the cedars drink
slow fire under the sod.
A flame seeps up the core,—

a tall tree falls.
From the bark, the white smoke bleeds.
Midway between midnight and daybreak
the sky egg cracks across.
Goats move in sleep.
Night then speaks with one dry boom.
The goats veer in their steps and stir
fire-flies from live oak trees
with their small lightnings.
One horned beast trots from the herd
more in disdain than fright
into the open, a little distance foraging.
The old devil knows
despite that bright, slow, loud antiphon
it will not rain.

CANAL STREET

FOR SUSAN WATTS STREET

Venice, whose streets are wavering reflections
of leaning palaces and strips of sky,—
Byzantine water-lily where the Winged
Lion nested; your seed-pod domes have scattered
seeds of dome-capped towers over our cities
constructed of steel flames, whose streets are shade.
(Each tower is a web, spun by a spider
efficient, diligent) now through our caves of trade
aromas blow of pollen dust (choking,
exuberant) from your malicious dead:
our human Principalities and Powers
your Named and Nameless who are mixt with Fate.

THE HUNTSMAN

FOR LINCOLN EDWARD KIRSTEIN

My cartridge belt is empty.
I have killed no beasts.
I have one bullet.
Can we; with untrembled pistol
when a serpent clasps a child;
send the bullet through the serpent
past the small head of the child?
Be not disconsolate if the bullet
pierce both child and serpent.
A trembled pistol spares the serpent
to kill the child.
Throw the empty belt away.
Take the pistol.
Shoot

TO WISE MEN ON THE DEATH OF A FOOL

FOR MATTHEW JOSEPHSON

Wise men, when Crosby died, looked on each other
And saw musicians, who did not mistake
The catgut of their intruments for heart strings
Withered by necessary, if regretful, Life.

—Wise men, presented in self-portraiture—
Presume to hold your scales, like Rhadamanthus;
And weigh yourselves and Crosby; your own scales
(After due vacillations of the dart)
Will rest, to show your reassured eyes
A pound of lead outweigh a pound of feathers.
Crosby, in feathers, danced through a sealed house
Which he unsealed, whose Idol's cerements,
In ever-lessening spirals, he unwrapped
With helian desire to grasp the Sun.

*Address to men who
share similar judgments
for differing reasons*

*Crosby, the sunwor-
shipper*

41

Compared first to a
raven in a peacock's
plumes

And saw no sun, but saw the uncovered skull;
Shuddered upon a sharp and fleshless mouth;
And then, to warm his covered skeleton
Fired his borrowed feathers. A night bird
He blazed in plumes of smoke before the crowd.

and then with the
phoenix

A traveler once wrote home from Africa:
"I saw the fowl. But the time was out of season.
It was only a chick. And when young, the Phoenix
Is no more astounding than a barn-yard cock."

Wise men unworthy
of a cult for Crosby

Hierophants, turned neophytes, adore
This worshipper of Faithfulness in wolves,
Wisdom in doves and Gentleness in snakes.
Let not New England join, from whence he sprung
Towards which he looked, too eager to amaze,
And wondered, "What may Boston say about me
Now"; and dying, exulted, wondering "What
Can they now say?" State Street, maintain your silence.
His mad impiety is holier than your sane
Infidel doubt; but, you sane infidels
You wise men, named in Crosby's diary,
Whose words are linked with his words, be discreet
And please the financiers, who have exacted
Murder and suicide with Investment Council.

Crosby unworthy of
a cult.

Let men made easy by his death keep silent
Resenting Crosby's life, and Crosby's death
Resenting. Poetry has saints. He was not of them.
His death was his best poem, and Crosby, dead
Shall live in history, like the marauders
Infatuate of new-found luxuries
Who fired the scrolls of Alexandria
To warm the waters of the public baths.

Similar judgments
and dissimilar rea-
sons reconciled

Wise men, without regard to almanacs
Be amorous, opulent, inebriate
Penurious, abstinent and solitary.
Wise men are moon-gazers, who never challenge

42

The fisher of tides to mesh them in her net.
Wise men have built, with calm of Antonine
Their philosophic membrances, which absorb
From toxic chaos, only pleasing lies.

Magnanimous in bronze, and straddling a stallion
Over the Roman Capitol, diffusing
A green benediction, rides serene Aurelius.

SALVATION ARMY GIRL

FOR ROBERT FITZGERALD

A Salvation Army girl stands on the western
steps of a Cathedral Church, whose leathern doors
now open and now close, like tired chimes.
As stop-go lights transmit their messages
of danger and safety, her tireless, vocal eyes
speak, as voices speak to bells or drums.

"The City of God spreads out before me
here, in the western Babylon.
Heavenly Salem is here, amid fumes of Hell
where the streets lead to destruction.
I judge not abomination
by my faltering tongue, infallible.
Here, in my own thin lap
is the seat of abundant mercy.
Here, in the womb of the Scarlet Whore
lies the ever unborn, the ever virgin.
Here a fresh stream, for all who would drink
springs through the brine of the ocean."

Vernal notes drop down; while brazen tongues
chime, both eyes close; the high bells chime;
like feathered coins, the bells, or cherubim;
like maple seeds, the chimes, like autumn sunrise
bells fallen on her tambourine with coins;
and copper drum-taps startle icy bells.

43

Bear her, ye flaming bells and buoyant words
to the Gate of Swords (unlatched but guarded)
even as the war horse of devouring Faith
once carried Joan, the Maid
with stamping, foam and snorting,
docile beneath such timid mastery.

Hailing a truck, loaded with brick bats
and giving all her collection to the driver
a Salvation Army girl, openly at noon time
gathered an idle crowd of sailors
from the 10c bread line of the Cathedral soup kitchen
and 35c flop house.

—"I am a child of peace" she said.
My unfaltering tongue is fallible.
But if I were you, I would smash these painted
windows of the Justice of abomination
and break the abundant idols, carved
upon these Babylonian doors.
—Your damage to the Devil's property
would not count up to more than you have paid
begging and stealing, to maintain the right
of asking to be kept alive."

Bricks drop like bats. And smashing glass;
like thundering guns or chimes of money;
runs all heaped and scattering
like topsy-turvy tambourines of change
till silently, the mob dissolved from her.

—The total loss has not been figured
though the clergy spent the afternoon
pounding Cathedral adding machines.
—The Salvation Army girl, held for inciting to riot
is released on bond for psychopathic observation.
—General Evangeline feels no responsibility
and Captain Miles Standish tells our special correspondent
that he has always taken pains to get on pleasantly

with the Bishop and Trustees of the Cathedral Church
of Mary, the Star of the Sea.

FISH FOOD
AN OBITUARY TO HART CRANE

FOR MALCOLM COWLEY

As you drank deep as Thor, did you think of milk or wine?
Did you drink blood, while you drank the salt deep?
Or see through the film of light, that sharpened your rage with its stare,
a shark, dolphin, turtle? Did you not see the Cat
who, when Thor lifted her, unbased the cubic ground?
You would drain fathomless flagons to be slaked with vacuum—
The sea's teats have suckled you, and you are sunk far
in bubble-dreams, under swaying translucent vines
of thundering interior wonder. Eagles can never now
carry parts of your body, over cupped mountains
as emblems of their anger, embers to fire self-hate
to other wonders, unfolding white, flaming vistas.

Fishes now look upon you, with eyes which do not gossip.
Fishes are never shocked. Fishes will kiss you, each
fish tweak you; every kiss take bits of you away,
till your bones alone will roll, with the Gulf Stream's swell.
So has it been already, so have the carpers and puffers
nibbled your carcass of fame, each to his liking. Now
in tides of noon, the bones of your thought-suspended structures
gleam as you intended. Noon pulled your eyes with small
magnetic headaches; the will seeped from your blood. Seeds
of meaning popped from the pods of thought. And you fall. And the unseen
churn of Time changes the pearl-hued ocean;
like a pearl-shaped drop, in a huge water-clock
falling; from *came* to *go*, from *come* to *went*. And you fell.

Waters received you. Waters of our Birth in Death dissolve you.
Now you have willed it, may the Great Wash take you.
As the Mother-Lover takes your woe away, and cleansing

45

grief and you away, you sleep, you do not snore.
Lie still. Your rage is gone on a bright flood
away; as, when a bad friend held out his hand
you said, "Do not talk any more. I know you meant no harm."
What was the soil whence your anger sprang, who are deaf
as the stones to the whispering flight of the Mississippi's rivers?
What did you see as you fell? What did you hear as you sank?
Did it make you drunken with hearing?
I will not ask any more. You saw or heard no evil.

COME OVER AND HELP US
A RHAPSODY

FOR QUINCY HOWE

I

Our masks are gauze + and screen our faces for those unlike us only,
Who are easily deceived. + Pierce through these masks to our
        unhidden tongues
And watch us scold, + scold with intellectual lust; + scold
Ourselves, our foes, our friends; + Europe, America, Boston; and
        all that is not
Boston; + till we reach a purity, fierce as the love of God;— + Hate.
Hate, still fed by the shadowed source; + but fallen, stagnant fallen;
Sunk low between thin channels; rises, rises; + swells to burst
Its walls; and rolls out deep and wide. + Hate rules our drowning Race.
Any freed from our Tyrant; + abandon their farms, forsake their
        Country, *become American.*

We, the least subtle of Peoples, + lead each only one life at a time,—
Being never, never anything but sincere; + yet we trust our honesty
So little that we dare not depart from it,— + knowing it to need
        habitual stimulation.
And living amid a world of Spooks, + we summon another to us
Who is (in some sort) our Clown,— + as he affords us amusement.
O! sweet tormentor, Doubt! longed-for and human, + leave us
        some plausible
Evil motive, however incredible. + The Hate in the World
        outside our World
(Envious, malicious, vindictive) + makes our Hate gleam in the splendor
Of a Castrate + who with tongue plucked out; + arms, legs sawed off;
Eyes and ears, pierced through; + still thinks + thinks
By means of all his nutriment, + with intense, exacting Energy,
        terrible, consuming.
Madness, we so politely placate + as an every-day inconvenience
We shun in secret. + Madness is sumptuous; Hate, ascetic.
Those only who remain sane, + taste the flavor of Hate.
Strong Joy, we forbid ourselves + and deny large pleasurable objects,

47

But, too shrewd to forego amusement, + we enjoy all joys which,
　　　　　　　　　　　　　　　　　　dying, leave us teased.
So spare us, sweet Doubt, our tormentor, + the Arts, our concerts,
　　　　　　　　　　　　　　　　　　　　　　　and novels;
The theater, sports, the exotic Past; + to use to stave off Madness,
To use as breathing spells, + that our drug's tang may not die.
We are not tireless; + distract us from thin ecstasy, that we may hate
If with less conviction, + with some result, some end,—
So pure ourselves; so clear our passion; + *pure, clear, alone.*

II

The New Englander leaves New England + to flaunt his drab person
Before Latin decors + and Asiatic back-drops.
Wearies. + Returns to life,—life tried for a little while.
A poor sort of thing + (filling the stomach; emptying the bowels;
Bothering to speak to friends on the street; + filling the stomach again;
Dancing, drinking, whoring) + forms the tissue of this fabric.—
(Marriage; society; business; charity;— + *Life, and life refused.*)

The New Englander appraises sins, + finds them beyond his means,
　　　　　　　　　　　　　　　　　　　　+ and hoards.
Likewise, he seldom spends his goodness + on someone ignoble as he,
But, to make an occasion, he proves himself + that he is equally ignoble.
Then he breaks his fast! + Then he ends his thirsting!
He censors the Judge. + He passes judgment on the Censor.
　　　　　　　　　　　　　　　　+ No language is left.
His lone faculty, Condemnation,—condemned. + Nothing is left to say.
Proclaim an Armistice + Through Existence, livid, void, + *let silence flood.*

Ask the Silent One your question. + (He is stupid in misery
No more than the talkative man, who talks through his hat.) + Ask
　　　　　　　　　　　　　　　　　　　　the question.
If he replied at all, + it would be to remark that he never could despise
Anyone so much as himself + should he once give way to Self-pity.
A different act of faith is his,— + the white gesture of Humility.
He knows his weakness. + He is well-schooled + and he never
　　　　　　　　　　　　　　　　　　forgets the shortest

Title of his Knowledge. ✦ The jailer of his Soul sees Pride. He sees
Tears, never. ✦ The Silent One is so eaten away
He cannot make that little effort ✦ which surrender to external Fact
Requires, ✦ but looks out always with one wish,— ✦ *to realize he exists.*

Lo! a Desire! ✦ A Faint motive! ✦ A motive (however faint)
                                                    beyond disinterestedness.
Faint. ✦ It is faint. ✦ But the boundary is clear. ✦ Desire, oh desire further!
Past that boundary lies Annihilation ✦ where the Soul
Breaks the monotonous-familiar ✦ and man wakes to the shocking
Unastounded company of other men. ✦ But the Silent One would not pass
Where the Redmen have gone. ✦ He would live without end.
                            That,— ✦ *the ultimate nature of Hell.*

GESTURES TO THE DEAD

FOR PERSONS NAMED THEREIN

I

Do valleys faint to view the exhausted hills?
The sun, desire wasted long ago,
now fructifies the earth with cooling duty;
but Uncle Sam divorced Columbia
to moon in Whimsy-land, with Columbine.
Does Santa Claus believe in Ponce de Leon?
Would Michael splinter his two-handed sword
and pare the sable wings of Azrael?
Let him take warning from the stone box where
Woodrow Wilson lies, still as Charlemagne
under heaps of Gothic architecture.
Fill, Angel, fill with the unholy thrill
of an illustrated, Benzoidal lecture,—
and hand us down your silver trumpet, Gabriel.
Do choirs of Heaven weary of Heaven's Court?
For Seraph and Cherub, do love and knowledge stale?
St. James' Court enjoyed James Russell Lowell
because he wrote no *Government of England*.
Yet Lawrence Lowell was never made ambassador
although he stalwartly condemned Vanzetti.

What a pity Amy was not President of Harvard!
What a pity Anarchists tried to frighten Yankees!
Needles of law pierced the blindfolded eyes
of Justice; and the eyes flowed in tears and blood.
Maybe the Judge's secretary knew
the judge believed the culprits innocent.
But innocent of jurisprudence, innocent
of clemency (while "Bohes" became publicists
by making thumbnoses) stalwart Lawrence Lowell
(the memory of the deed can never fade)
condemned two men to death because the *Transcript*
held not in all its files their alibi,—
a wop clam-bake at Plymouth (or was it Quincy?)

All male Quincys are now dead, excepting one.
Yes, all Heaven's servants see their tasks are hopeless;
yet out the burning cavern of deep space
an aching and weary whip scourges our backs
and, through the shuddering All, rolls the command: "Go on."

Each Chamber of Commerce manufactures
its own Five-Year-Plan;
a super-power plant has shaken
the Palace of the Vatican;
Neo-Thomists and not engineers
should meet in consultation,
while the Apostolic Radio
weeps for the Workingman.
Go on, Go on, Slavic Boy Scouts.
Two blades of grass grow where one grew before.
U.S.S.R. and U.S.A. Y.M.C.A.?
Go on, Go on, from strength to strength.

Bigger and better. Bigger and better.

II

Economists, who cultivate statistics;
to prove the truth of economic destiny
by your complete obedience to its laws;—
Our youth prepares our minds to recollect
our memories of history while we live.
All dead men live now among living men.
The savage, the Nile man, Euphrates man,
the Apollonian, Dionysian Greek,
Etrurian corporation lawyer.
Mosaic Arab and Jew of the Diaspora,
the Apostolic, Patristic, Byzantine,
Nordic, Barbarian, Pagan, anchorite
and monk of the Dark Ages, who rakes embers
to set the woods on fire behind his back,
Burgher, Crusader, Prince of athletic virtue,
Conquistador; Elizabethan pirate,

State-minded bigot, Baroque casuist,
Sceptic, Deist, Conservative, Agnostic;—

who has not all of these for friends confines
his love of drama to the costume play.
He could not sit through Hamlet in plain clothes.
He dooms his sons to be low-pressure salesmen.
One, who in reading Plato does not hear
his friends rehearse characteristic thought
should add new leaves and clasps to his address book.
He needs to clean the beeswax from his ear.

For this, I recommend a woman's hairpin.

III

Does she who rules the sea rule the Thesaurus?
And must the tide of adolescent rage,
which floods philosophy into the mind,
recede as one grows old and words come slow?
I have an hour-glass of years in my
receding hair. Burke's hair is gray.
But we have pimples that blossom with the Spring.
The destinies of thinkers are quick words
which come between themselves and their slow thought.
Socratic knowledge of processes of knowing
is now distilled to a maxim of cold poison:
"Know thyself." Do you prefer the ant-like
Freud to the bearded Leonardo, weaver
of all the web of knowing, but self-knowledge?

William James lies in a broadcloth box
with silver handles, Pragmatism, three
syllables beginning with a P.
His father said that he found Swedenborg
fairly insipid with veracity.
Are all the wheeling ages turned as vain
as the flutter of these sages' paper prayers?
No, never, while the quintessential charm;

"I, I, the It, Self, I,
Who, where, when and why?"

of Mary Baker Eddy, Sorceress, stands; and it shall stand!

IV

The stars and planets weary of ether wind
and weary of their own, their endless song.
Their praise of heaven thrills not as when it rolled
forth when the sky was young, ere Ezra Pound
proclaimed: Pianos are percussion instruments.
And can poets hunger for the wind no longer
as hungered spirits, gone a different way?
Shelley, who was too much like thee, O Wind.
The pard-like spirit, who said that he was pard-like.
Spirits who did not call themselves bad names
in public print, as T. S. Eliot did:
Classicist, Royalist, Anglo-Catholic,
long names for the four letter word, a snob.
Why, when a writer totters out of fashion
are we reminded how his life is sad?

Cossacks of criticism, æsthetic bloodhounds:
All life is sad. Welcome the evil fortunes
of sad dressmakers for the soul in mourning.
They are glad portents of Furies and the Muses.
Let pity be confined to boarding-schools
where, by the Church's discipline, small boys
are turned to beautifully deformed bond salesmen.
(Did ever a nation's manhood all turn pimps?)
Were ever a nation's poets made great by pity?
Pity is foreign to the love of truth.
Let bondsmen pity them, who, in young manhood
criticise critics of criticism
and edit critics, methodologically.
And I, who wasted all my early youth
by talking about God to older women
once pondered long upon American critics!

Then pity me, and hear the truths I learned:
The coral aisles of art have shifting sand-bars.
Do editors think sand-bars *terra firma*?

Deep in his soul a good man, slowly wise
felt the devouring need to edit something.
During his pilgrimage through Humanism,
gazing, by the lagoon, on his moustache
he met a sight, more dignified in his eyes
than in the eyes of the undignified
who play in the surf and clamber cliffs beyond
Gorham B. Munson, a second Parsifal.

Nietzsche said *Carmen* was the greatest opera.

V

As Tate grows old some child will fondle him
as his mother's children fondled grandpapa.
Be resolute, for there is no solution;
as I grow old, dark slumber fades to gray.
Ulysses Grant fought for the Constitution
and chewed his old cigars while it whirled over
the piazza steps, into an ancient dump-cart
where films of dust so lightly lie upon
Constantine's Declaration of Independence.
Habeas corpus, requiescat in pace.
Booth evaded the fame he sought, by speaking
justly of Lincoln, *sic semper tyrannis.*
It was banal enough to be immortal.
You, Judas, sacrificed for our Messiah.
You, Brutus, needful for our Caesar cult.
Yours is the signal deed of all our history
for pure liberty, for freedom, not reform.
Some men fight Fate with its own fatal weapons,
and ever believe they kill themselves for the life
of the thing they kill, as Lincoln died for the Union.

Others who fail find that no path lies open

but the bridle-path of remaining dignified.
It took Robert E. Lee three days to become a "traitor,"
and he rode to his gray end, a college president.
When men of action fail, and failing, ask
sanctuary of thinkers, destiny rests.
There is nothing more to say. Can Tate and I
stand against the black drift of storm

forever changeless, against a changing sky?

GENERAL ARGUMENT

The title of this book prepares for the mental play and organization with which the author would provide his readers, hoping that the heavy poems are fine in structure and the light poems as firm as they.

This book contains all the author's verse which has been published since the appearance of *Eight More Harvard Poets* (Brentano's) 1923. He thanks the editors of *The Advocate*; *The American Caravan IV* (Macaulay Company) 1931; *Contempo*; *The Dragon*; *The Hound and Horn*; *Housatonic*; *The Little Review*; *The New Republic*; *The Outlander*; *Poetry, a Magazine of Verse*; *Secession*; *The Sewanee Review*; and *Smoke* for their publication of poems which are here now reprinted or revised. He thanks those to whom he dedicates the book and the poems, or whom he mentions in this general argument, for their assistance to the work. Subsequent volumes may afford opportunity to acknowledge other debts. Above all, the author thanks S. Foster Damon, his brother-in-law, and in letters.

Readers may use the arguments to these pieces either as inducements or as limits to further interpretation. On a symbolic poem, as on a clothes horse, many persons hang many things. Yet the value of symbolic poems may be judged as much by the number of meanings which cannot be put upon them as by the rigidity with which they can sustain the meanings to which they are susceptible. Their words are transcendentally intended plot for any characters who obey.

NORTH ATLANTIC PASSAGE quotes the Hymnal, the Psalter, the Bhagavad Gita, Oliver Wendell Holmes, Stonewall Jackson, and an anonymous ejaculation made at the Jamestown Flood. Note that generally throughout this version of the poem, Enigmas are called "you"; Authority is called "he". The Senses, the Reason and the Spirit may be distinguished by the use of the respective pronouns "thou" "I" and "they". Reference to the Soul is made by the use of "we".

INCEPTION OF THE CROSS attached itself to a saying of Henry James' Ralph in the *Portrait of a Lady*. Readers who look in poetry for psychological data may care to know, that whether unreasonably or not, this, with the couple following, took their departure from the same occurrence.

The first draft of FORTY DAYS was written under Le Baron Russell Briggs after reading Baring-Gould's *Lost and Hostile Gospels* to which Ronald Levinson introduced the author. He owes his acquaintance with Apocryphal Christian literature to Kirsopp Lake and George Foote Moore at a time when he was young in the Anglican Communion for which Emily and John Diman, James O. S. Huntington, Spence Burton and Frederic Fitts prepared him. The poem deals with the season which falls between Christ's rising from the grave and his mounting from the earth. Alan Pope suggested the present reading of the closing strophe.

An old suggestion of Kenneth Burke's pushed the form of the opening section on from where it rested in earlier versions. Now the order of the aphorisms moves the hands of the clock backward at intervals throughout the dialogue. But although the discourse is in distorted sequence, a table to the normal passage of time is given in verses which note the behavior of beasts and plants and the progress of the sun, and interrogative refrains as well mark off sections of consecutive dialogue. Within these sections answers are given out before the questions to call them forth, and consequences are told in advance of their causes. Thus are the harangues supplied with plot, after the enigmatic formulas of mystery stories. The purpose of this machinery is not merely to give shock to aphorism but to accentuate the pertinence of one idea to another by apparent logical isolation. The uses of poetry are: to sound, to show, to teach. Whereas the first two of these has lately undergone complex clarification, now the didactic, if it is to assume its place with them, must undergo proportionate handling.

Many uncanonical sayings of Jesus preserved by the Fathers' refutation of false constructions long put upon them, are consistent with Gospel sayings; and this uncanonical wisdom, in the author's ear, recovers for systematic Christianity moral qualities which Quietists now leave to Sceptics. The author takes for the basis of his prosodic statement of faith, these germs of act, seeds to split rock.

No mere inertia causes the Church to try saints and authoritatively mistake God for the Devil, but an active hostility whose weapons of war condemn life by formulas which sanctify death. The living Crucified's discourse to the recalcitrant Church precipitated into act; first on his own part, then by contagion among his fellow men; is in its aim without concern for any worldly consequence. The Word in its passage through society assails the Father of Lies and False Witness by forces which are allied only loosely with earthly revolution, but which lead those who hear to inexorable rebellion against injustice. It is at once a ground for Faith and Doubt that

57

decent behavior or opinion is not distinguishable from sedition, even as what is taken for stale dogma turns out to be fresh truth.

WHY MUST YOU KNOW? is written in two voices,—whether of the same mind or of different persons. The second voice speaks throughout WOULD YOU THINK?

MOSSY MARBLES is a literal contradiction to Oliver Wendell Holmes' *The Voiceless.*

TWILIGHT, a dramatic narrative of pragmatic repression, is the first of three completed workings of a mine of material in Walker's translation of a Nestorian novel on the Acts of Thomas. This Paraphrase clarifies the original where, as in any good entertainment, the persons of the piece are aspects of one mind. The author owes the strophe of the bride's discovery to Theodore Spencer. The author states for the guidance of some conceivable reader who may be fatuous enough to suppose for any length of time that the love song towards the close of this piece is intended to be an exercise in spiritual beauty,—that it is not.

From the first hint the author learned that the doubting Apostle was the Apostle to India, he was moved by its implications; from which other implications spread as he learned that Thomas is a word for twin, Didymos, that this Apostle was called the brother of the Lord, and that, like Iscariot and Simon the Anti-Christ, his name was Judas.

PAUL AND VIRGINIA is in memory of a West Medford garden, the most splendid of Massachusetts, where the author spent the summers of early childhood. Even as it was built of profits from the exploitation of the sea, so it has long since been destroyed by profit-seeking exploitation of the land. The fact that its fate was its appropriate destiny gives no comfort to them who loved it and who, with its vanishing, found themselves deprived, as by a racial blood-letting, of the body of their cultural inheritance. These same Statues are hero and heroine in Amy Lowell's *Legends,* "The Statue in the Garden."

PLANTATION DROUGHT; written in Dean Hall, Strawberry, near Charleston, South Carolina; was induced as much by an economic as by the atmospheric barometer.

CANAL STREET depends at first upon a sonnet of Henry Wadsworth Longfellow's and closes with a line of James Russell Lowell's.

THE HUNTSMAN grew from the Greek Anthology to a dilemma in revolutionary desire.

TO WISE MEN ON THE DEATH OF A FOOL has as its hero a poet who is the subject of poems by Crane and Cummings. The unfortunate Crosby, just when his technical facility might mirror his devotion to his art, put an end to his days by a luxurious crime. His moral philosophy explains his behavior, for he took the symbology of Decadence pragmatically to heart rather than in some sensorial sense, which is far more appropriate. The Decadent school of literature relies upon the logic of the implied paradox to endow the aesthetic with a vitality equivalent to that of morals. Crosby tried to live art rather than, even, to live for art which is, as a profession, quite dangerous enough. His perilous experiment farced life and verse. His mind suffered from impediments implanted there by the code of manners under which he was reared. The mock society into which he was born had emasculated him. It seeks to emasculate every male child. In the name of all that is called wholesome it shields its young from an early impact with the whole force of culture, that they may forever be concerned only with destructive busying in stocks and bonds, or at worst in publishing. But culture takes a terrible vengeance upon its victims. Long and effectively has this mock society conducted itself by ignoring the fact that men's comprehension of matters of the mind chiefly distinguishes them from women. Poor Crosby, denied the tutelage of Chiron and confined too early and late in the Megaron, was not man enough to be a poet. Yet, in some deeper sense a son of Pelops than by grace of breeding, he is a hero fit for eulogy. Now-a-days no one can claim to fame who does not at some point war against the hostility to manhood which at all points presses upon imaginative work. Harry Crosby died for this.

THE SALVATION ARMY GIRL, although only a fancied person, felt very much in this way, and, although she came from the lower class to her conviction while Crosby came only from the upper class, she accomplished as little as he. The unrest of Lollards and Levelers bubbled up in her and was sluiced through the unscientific channel her religious ancestors provided.

FISH FOOD, an Obituary to Hart Carne, employs a six beat meter. In the Norse Fable of how Thor arriving in the dead of night at a lonely cabin, weary and in need of drink and warmth, found there an old woman sitting by a big flagon of ale at her fireside with a cat; and how he gulped down the ale without, mighty drinker, being able to drain the flagon and budged the cat from the best place by the hearth without, strong wrestler, being able to quite displace her; then to learn upon waking that as he drank from the flagon the level of the whole ocean had lowered, and that when he lifted the cat from off three paws he had dislodged the tortoise who holds up the earth, and the earth had slipped a little from its accustomed place, the author takes the flagon to be the infinite of conceivable sensation and the cat to be the universe of possible act. Crane took little interest in the cat and vowed himself to the flagon—he drank more than his fill, and was overwhelmed by the ale fumes. Perhaps in ending his life he caused his country trouble; for the power of his resentment against established facts, which he drove inward, would, when the inward had proved an inadequate foe, have directed itself outward against foes no less vulnerable than himself—foes more worthy of hatred. He would have assailed injustices, if not in treasonable act, then certainly in literary equivalents, and embers of subversive sentiment. The author, though a bad friend, contributes these verses to Crane's accumulating fame.

COME OVER AND HELP US; written in Blake's seven beat epic meter, which was first analyzed by S. Foster Damon; a rhapsody upon the type Bostonian, embodies in part the author's response to the case of Sacco and Vanzetti during the latter year of whose trial it was composed. Yankee Hate, whose shadowed source is individual predestination turned secular, takes on corporate personality now and again in chauvinism; but is otherwise dominant only as it weakens separate selfish minds. These minds are faulty membranes between their persons and exterior events. They break down in active madness or they turn to callous prisons in passive solipsism,—at least such is the thesis of this poem.

The Macedonian salutation to the Apostles was placed by the author's father upon his pier-house at City Point, Boston, because it was used in the establishment of Puritan Commonwealths at home and abroad. As the title for his poem, it is addressed to the world that is not Boston.

GESTURES TO THE DEAD presents cosmic verses from the author's final piece in *Eight More Harvard Poets* in juxtaposition with verses political, historic, philosophic, aesthetic, metaphysical, with but little rational sequence. The method of an intuitive logic, now frequently used for the sensorial, is here used with ideas,—see Byron.

JOHN WHEELWRIGHT

Yaddo 1933

MIRRORS OF VENUS
A NOVEL IN SONNETS
1914-1938

ARGUMENT

'...post hoc, ergo propter hoc...'

The Sonnet weds thought form to verse form within a compass little extended beyond the span of instinctive thought. A sonnet is a figure eight inverted (8). The "perfect" sonnet (like the first and tenth numbers of this Sequence) would have one major and two minor turns. Larger turns develop sequences. As the sonnet structure conforms inwardly to dialectic reasoning and outwardly to the Golden Mean, a sonnet sequence should rise to grandeur.

But when by defect of skill the outward form serves as a bed of Procrustes rather than as a bed of Hymen, any sonnet is discomforting. When, with habitual knack in versifying or with superstitious shunning of all but conventional thoughts or notions, a poet comes across with "perfect" sonnet after "perfect" sonnet for any length of time, a sonnet sequence is a bore.

Poets waste their energy who contrive how to induce hypnosis by monotony which readers in their turn must resist if they are to get more than jingles from their reading. Rather should poets spend their melodic skill to put their thoughts into relief. This, the original intention of sonnets, is frustrated by sequences outwardly less varied than *The New Life* of Dante, which includes among its sonnets a ditty, two fragments, and three canzone. It is debatable whether or not all verses with the thought form of an inverted figure eight (8) and only such verses should be called sonnets; but it is beyond question that sonnets and sonnets inverted and distorted can enliven each other and make a long sequence pleasantly intelligible.

Not varied rhyme schemes to Petrarch's sestet, nor Michael Angelo's use of coda and double coda; neither distortions of Petrarch's octave rhyme scheme, nor Milton's distortions of the inner form—none of these devices if long extended can prevent deadening monotony. Spenser's or Shakespeare's new-forged schemes are shocks at first, but they induce by custom and at long last even deeper hypnosis. While alternation between Petrarch's, Shakespeare's, even Milton's forms cannot save a sequence from vitiation, a whole sequence of sonnets in free verse would display the thought forms themselves in a skeletal monotony which prosody purposes to disguise. Sonnets in free verse are of use to punctuate conventional sequence and are of greater use when their introduction serves by contrast to make distorted forms approximate conventional effect. They are so used in this Sequence.

What may well seem elliptical syntax, logical incoherence, and inequivalence in the branches of simile were ordered through revisions for more than twenty years to give the performance such faults as conventional performances lack.

The rhymes are marked in the margin of the text with numerals in order to spare those who may be interested in technical analysis from that gymnastic turning of horizontal into vertical which one must go through to follow even so simple a statement as: the octave is rhymed: a, b, b, a; b, a, a, b; and the sestet: c, d, d; c, c, d. The thought-turns of the Sequence are indicated on the Table of Contents and by the serial numbers of the separate Arguments because they are of more than technical importance. Within framing Laments and Elegies they mark Chapters in this Novel whose plot, though built upon digression, relates: first, that the death of a friend prevented the death of a friendship; and second, that the survivor grew in faith from Immortal Selfhood to Eternal Solidarity. Arguments are printed below the text rather than at the end of the book in order to avoid thumbing the leaves back and forth. Readers of these Arguments will bear in mind that it is impossible to say a poem over in prose and that any poem means something more and something else than its author meant. The signification of the title is that (as in Burne-Jones' picture) the mirror of Venus reflects loved ones as each would be seen.

The numbers of this Sequence are for the late Ned Couch; the Harvard Class of 1920; Lloyd K. Garrison; Quincy Howe; my Father, the late Ned Wheelwright; my Saviour; Horace Howard Furness Jayne; Leonard Opdycke; James Agee; Fairfield Porter; Emlin Paul Etting; the late Frederic Jones; William Slater Brown; Robert Fitzgerald; Robert Hillyer, to whose example the Sequence owed much; and to Richardson King Wood, who was its inception.

MIRRORS OF VENUS

Chapter One
LAMENTS

Death   Movie Show
And for his Mother   Link

Chapter Two
THE SEQUENCE

Abel   Flux
Adam   Sophomore
Sanct   Classmates
Heat and Cold   Mother

Chapter Three

Father   Lens
Rococo Crucifix   Eye-Opener
Holy Saturday

Chapter Four

Week End Bid I   Kin
Week End Bid II   Venus and Bacchus
Sabotage   Minus
Plus

Chapter Five

Spider   Phallus
Parting in Harlem   Keeper
Village Hangover   Mirror
Get-Away

Chapter Six
ELEGIES

Spring   Autumn
Summer   Winter

LAMENTS

*

DEATH AT LEAVENWORTH

Perhaps a lot of you have lost a friend,—
a friend who had a way of saying things
you can't remember, yet you can't forget,—
things which make you almost weep for more
now that you know that more can never come,—
a friend not made to die till the chrysalis
of sense peeled from him and his sixth sense learned
it had been born to supra-sensual moths.

> Out there at Leavenworth that bored you;
> shy at you shoulder-strap; back among friends;
> and then Across;—"An overdose of morphine"?
> That is absurd. Mere doctors could not kill
> a soldier who detested war, a soldier
> thus self-inoculated against death.
>   Ned. Ned.
> Why, after twenty years, do I think you killed yourself?

I

is the first of four LAMENTS *which draw the reader from the world of prose through blank verse to rhyme.* Trust in the Immortal Self together with trust in undying love forms the positive theme of the whole work.

AND FOR HIS MOTHER

For your own mother, you remain Baby
jumping to give her (crumpled in crumpled fist)
a baby dandelion, green and gold.
But, as now and again, when tipsy friends plumb deeps
of conversation unexpressed, you came
to hover over the home-brew, and then spoke
in random piano notes some fellow made
to ornament his wit. Your mild eyes gleamed
      with scorn to beg for an immortal selfhood
      and warm blood, humming underneath cool skin
      clear as October evening, flooded all
      your vernal frailty with fury. Streams
      of sympathy pour over distant height
      dispassionately intimate in death.

II

Faith in the Immortal Self drops to the hallucination of personal
persistence after death.

MOVIE SHOW

Through slow tobacco smoke, once more a flush
runs over those cheek bones' pale quick smile
and you are off with books under your arm . . .

Some day, perhaps, when all your friends have left
their seats for strangers; you'll leave this movie house
and have, outside in the fresh air, other pleasure.
Will your friends "hello" you; will they bear you
toward gentian evening water, there to hear
a Voice that walks beneath apple trees . . .?
                        Or, first dead friend,
        is the Communion of Latter Saints to find
        annihilation, immortality
        and our salvation in oblivion?

III

gives out in its Coda a loss of faith in the Immortal Self which, together
with a loss of trust in undying friendship, will form the negative theme
of the work.

LINK

Had you not died, our friendship might be dead   1
for the world it was born to died in war   2
and may drag on only in avatar;   2
yet how I wish you lived, and that instead   1
of you, all our affection had been laid   1
away and, holding memory's lens, we saw   2
friendship's morphology in perfect law   2
who reckoned when our friendship might be dead.   1

Not only I were livelier had you lived   3
work-mate to lay a morbid culture's ghost;   4
but you yourself embalmed, beatified   5
in friendship's reliquary, and I shrived   3
in love's confessional, where love is lost   4
as our love would be lost, had you not died.   5

IV

is conventional, except for its "Boston rhyme" of "war" and "law" and the weaving of its refrain.

THE SEQUENCE

★

ABEL

In the dead night we walk behind a hearse   1
zigzagging towards a dancing colonnade;   2
knee-deep, through dust of faded petals wade   2
past thornless flowers through thorns. Hear us converse: 1
"Whom do we mourn?" you ask me, half afraid.   2
"I mourn for you, and whom I mourn, I curse."   1
And, though I know my answer is perverse,   1
I do not know who the one was who prayed.   2

With dawn comes knowledge. The prophet in the fane   3
withered the valedictory spray we brought,   4
and swept it out into the empty court.   4
By scorn in love, by charity in disdain,   3
our fragmentary fealties attain   3
foreknowledge of the vacancy he sought.   4

V (1 a)

records a dream of dying friendship where Y and Z walk in Y's funeral.
X, who is always present with friends, rejects their votive offering. The
verse "zigzagging towards a dancing colonnade" recalls the pleasure
of watching in architecture the kinetic performance of form against
form.

ADAM

Subject alone to lonely and sincere   1
allegiance to crown-and-robeless liberty, 2
he can submit to no authority,—   2
yet he is wise in all he does revere,   1
and lovable, because his will is clear   1
and beautiful, because his mind is free. 2
In him, all admirable traits appear   1
and he is kindly, for he owns no fear.   1

 A youthful Adam, fresh from Genesis, 3
 standing in memory, with pectoral muscles bright 4
 alabaster, dusted by morning's light; 4
 comprised the Sodomites' antithesis,— 3
 and, could I be as he looked in my sight, 4
 from friendship would arise a trinity. 2

VI (1 b)

describes and praises the presence between friends. *The distorted rhyme
scheme of the octave, deferring the fourth recurrence of the second rhyme until
the last of the sestet, throws the thought back and forward.*

SANCT

We know the Love the Father bears the Son   1
is a third Mask and that the Three form One.   1
We also know, machines and dynamos   2
—Preservers in motion; Destroyers in repose—   2
like visions of wheeled eyes the addict sees   3
are gods, not fashioned in our images.   3

Thus let us state the unknown in the known: 4
The mechanism of our friendship, grown   4
transcendent over us, maintains a being   5
by seeing us when we grow lax in seeing,   5
although without our sight it could not be.   6
(One states, one does not solve, a mystery.)   6
This human Trinity is comprehended   7
when doubt of its divinity has ended.   7

VII (1 c)

Friendship is contrasted with inorganic and compared to divine mechanism. *These couplets form the first of the inverted sonnets.*

HEAT AND COLD

Once we seemed neighbors; like two patient ledges 1
or furry citizens of wood and field 2
at midnight, when the lunar dawn revealed 2
savin trees over flowered blueberry hedges 1
whence our long shadow, from a swollen moon 3
traversed pastures to herald our approach. 4
Across night's mound the fading planets wheeled; 2
thickly the chilly grass was overstrewn 3
with strawberries we trampled. Ill concealed 2
behind my tongue, all my affection stirred; 5
between my lips, only a mocking word 5
that dried my palate with pulvery self-reproach. 4

I feared the heat of light I could not see, 6
and silence as sufficient colloquy. 6

VIII (2a)

Z brings to a countryside by night the fear and distrust that kill friendship. *Two sestets are knotted by a final couplet.*

73

FLUX

Amphibian, who feared the Nemesic eddy   1
of a waterfall where you would be already   1
merged indistinguishably with the dæmonic   2
flux or unfluxed rainbow, where proved unready   1
for your iridiation by brief, laconic   2
smirks. The elements are sparingly sardonic;   2
life and oblivion with them are the same;   3
    and he who'll have a posthumous presence sturdy   1
    enough to cast shadow from glinting fame,   3
    or his "Collected Works" architectonic   2
    enough to evoke at the mere mention of his name   3
    amid life's dissonances, one symphonic   2
    theme, dives through fear of oblivion with cleaving aim.   3

IX (2 b)

Z brings to a countryside by day an evasive reason why he distrusts Y.
*The second rhyme of the "octave" of seven verses becomes by dissonance the
first rhyme of the sestet.*

SOPHOMORE

Did no unseen pods cling to your coat by the river   1
boarding school, your innocence last wandered   2
when its long remembering had lain fallow   3
within my mind? That ghostly weed which burred   2
you was a me of me, unrecognized;   4
my college self who found others were shallow: 3

When, catching his own glance, he analyzed   4
what stared so impolitely from the mirror,   1
he wondered if he earnestly despised   4
that callow face; or did he hold it dearer   1
because, unlike his classmates, he preferred   2
talk with autumnal women, ever mellow,   3
or boys, with whom his well-considered word   2
not always marked him as a crazy fellow?   3

X (3a)

makes, with its paired sonnet, a figure eight on figure eight inverted (8 on 8). The discipline of self-distrust, based upon the common sense that he resembles his fellows whom he distrusts, may help Y to overcome what Z distrusts in him. *The sestet has rhymes so light as to be almost blank until the turn.*

CLASSMATES

Their naked, small ambitions are disgusting.   1
They prize the world's poor business more than peace.   2
They have no virtue but their looks. Encrusting   1
their speech with filth, they are senilities.   2
Waiting for age to make him less uncouth   3
he dared condemn, too harshly, their conceit;   4
and, blaming their inevitable youth,   3
condemned himself as well, and owns—defeat.   4

    That clown, incarcerate beyond release   2
    in the dark, floorless cell of self-distrusting   1
    foregoes remorse, dies by austerities   2
    and suffers Hell, that I may face my feet   4
    from amphitheatred towns of antique ease   2
    toward desert fastnesses whence brute truth stalks abroad.   3

XI (3 b)

*The conventional octave is not followed by the Shakesperian continuation of
the quatrain scheme and final couplet. The first of these rhyme schemes was
raveled at the start, the second is knitted at the close.* The sentiment moves
from distrust to assurance.

MOTHER

Dame Nature is no less a snob than we   1
for she discriminates between her friends,   2
imposing variously for varied ends   2
the limits on her wide benignity.   1
In her, not our own kindly mother see;   1
but, rather, a strange hostess, who unbends   2
upon occasion, occasionally sends   2
her invitations,—"quite informally."   1

     I do not mean to cast, hereby, reflection   3
     on the Darwinian Theory of Selection;   3
     nor to ridicule the Pathetic Fallacy;   1
     but only to point out the different status,   4
     the obvious, intellectual hiatus   4
     between snobbism by fresh ponds, and by a sea.   1

XII (4)

In nature Z finds the snobbism which causes him to distrust himself and others, and which he distrusts in Y. *The rhyme scheme is conventional except that the romantic rhyme of the octave is repeated as the second rhyme of the sestet.*

FATHER

An East Wind asperges Boston with Lynn's sulphurous brine.   1
Under the bridge of turrets my father built,—from turning sign   1
of CHEVROLET, out-topping our gilt State House dome   2
to burning sign of CARTER'S INK,—drip multitudes   3
of checker-board shadows. Inverted turreted reflections   4
sleeting over axle-grease billows, through all directions   4
cross-cut parliamentary gulls, who toss like gourds.   3

   Speak. Speak to me again, as fresh saddle leather   5
   (Speak; talk again) to a hunter smells of heather.   5
   Come home. Wire a wire of warning without words.   3
   Come home and talk to me again, my first friend. Father,   5
   come home, dead man, who made your mind my home.   2

XIII (5)

The first minor turn of the *Sequence* passes from citified nature to a city scene and to serious from playful thought. X, who has been compared to a prophet, to Adam, to the Third Person of the Trinity, and whose good intention Z has followed with parental concern for Y's death as a friend, is addressed through the person of Z's own dead father. *The Alexandrine meter makes up a total measure of seventy-two feet though this sonnet lacks two verses of the conventional quota. The second rhyme is far split to keep the ear expectant for the false rhyme on 3.*

ROCOCO CRUCIFIX

Guarded by bursts of glory, golden rays,—   1
Christ, when I see thee hanging there alone   2
in ivory upon an ebon throne,   2
like Pan, pard-girded, chapleted with bays;   1
I kiss thy mouth, I see thee in a haze,   1
but not of tears, and not the briar crown . . .   2
Is it, O Sufferer, my heart is stone?   2
Am I, in truth, the Judas who betrays?   1

    To hang in shame above a gory knoll,   3
    to die of scorn upon a splintered pole,—   3
    this was not beautiful, I know, for thee . . .   4
    Would I have whispered upon Calvary,   4
    "An interesting silhouette, there, see!"   4
    while God groaned in the dark night of his soul?   3

XIV (6a)

contradicts the axiom and corollary of Keats, "Beauty is Truth: Truth, Beauty," and recalls the silence of God's Father when God died.

HOLY SATURDAY

"Am I, in truth, the Judas who betrays? 1
Is it, O Sufferer, my heart is stone?" 2
—This rhetoric indecently displays 1
the meanness of a spirit over-prone 2
to chant its litanies, to beg God atone 2
for poses in the cadence of self-praise 1
and, treasuring its poor pride, to bemoan 2
even frivolities in paraphrase. 1

  Is any Penitential Sacrament 3
  effective medicine for the inept, 4
  the subtle, the indomitably adept 4
  folly of being human? Grave of God! 5
  When most contrite, I am most platypod— 5
  Rise Christ! Give these feet wings! My need is exigent. 3

XV (6b)

is caught back in the treacherous self-distrust from which *Sophomore*
was delivered.

LENS

Must I become (who scrutinize the mutable   1
intelligence) to my own thought inscrutable   1
that I can think my truth no more dependent   2
on what is known of God; or the transcendent   2
fountain of Grace to take informing function,   3
but by anointing Me with stringent unction?   3

There is no sorrow as in the root of hope
that pays no debt but one that long was owed
it by the Creditor, who made and found life good.
Turn by an inward act upon the world!
An innocence like our Creator's faith
is younger than my doubt. You give it birth
who, seeing evil less veiling than clear rain,
see truth in thought as through a lens of air.

XVI (7)

A second deliverance, the balancing needle point of the Sequence, contrasts with VII and pairs with X and XI. *The sestet has heavy rhymes in couplets. The octave is not built on rhyme but on woven assonance and coupled dissonance.* Agnostic mood, the natural result of evangelical individualism, leaves the problem of evil to its divine originator as Z adopts the unmetaphysical view of life which attracts him to Y.

EYE-OPENER

The voice ascends, and gentler tread. The stair-   1
well echoes till my eyes and ear-drums fill   2
with your footfall and tenderer guttural.   2
Each tongue caught its say; but "We must reach   3
the Serpent-Bird who pushed on bound gloom,"   4
persistently continues through your search.   3
With kindly talk and step you left the room;   4
with abrupt, stern thump behind me, you breathe, "Here!"   1

    As at these brows' command argument stops,   5
    the gait and tongue turn gentler again   6
    and I let my mouth rest while my eyes open   6
    like sundown tingle through darkling retrospect.   7
    Although musics of earth, noise-hunted, fade   8
    I watch a sudden tread, which springs daybreak erect   7
    and stern, trap hunters hunted and afraid   8
    for their manhunt against persistent hopes.   5

XVII (8)

is not concerned with Z's moods, but with Y's recovery of social hope through Orozco's revolutionary conversion of Aztec mythology. *The schemes of the two equal parts are muted by false rhyme.*

Where a fallen farmhouse leaves a scar	1
on the pasture, with a bed of pansies	2
with blackberries, black as caviar,	1
and Queen Anne's lace, and the coarser tansies	2
(grown in the century gone by	3
to keep away the dread swamp fevers)	4
with heights below me, and the height on high	3
of Quaker Hill of the True Believers,—	4
I plow the grasses, and tread the thistles	5
expectantly wondering where you are,	1
and that you send postcards for my epistles;	5
I turn, wherever a meadow bird whistles,	5
to catch you coming, and hear your cry.	3

XVIII (9 a)

The major turn of the Sequence affords a light mood emphasized by a four-beat meter which insures that the first and third rhymes of the octaves sound when the quintets close.

WEEK END BID II

I rise in the morning and close my shutter   1
to sleep, while the Sun swings from East to West;   2
and at night, when my lamps burn low and sputter,   1
put my head to bed to give it a rest.   2
Come here and talk to me. My muse and your muse   3
shall walk the pasture while we sleep,   4
that while we are waking, your views and my views   3
may grow more common-sense and deep   5
    (while distant milk trains clang to the city)   5
    in almost every word we utter   1
    and if not deeper, perhaps more witty.   5
    Come. If you don't, that will be a pity.   5
    Come if you can. You can, if you choose.   3

XIX (9b)

continues the preceding.

84

SABOTAGE

Well, fellow, when you travel (by lands, by seas:	1		2
by air; at night or day) and know palace	3	4	5
or hovel where I might meet you there, you ease	1	3	2
away. You never could unravel the lies	4	1	6
you would prepare, if I should say how guys	3	4	6
had heard the cavil, and that you should beware	1	3	–
of my dismay far more than of your malice.	4	–	5

Why will you slip the meeting? I have no dreams	7		8
of you, no fears, no plea; yet you dread to face	9	10	11
my greeting. Is my suspicion true? It seems	7	9	8
to be. Dislikes and likes repeating, we'd sit	10	7	12
a whole day through; yet miserly in glut,	9	10	12
even to cheating yourself by a taboo	7	9	–
on company, you sap friendship's abundant base.	10	1	11

XX (9c)

embeds in its five-beat verses and final Alexandrine a counterpointed structure, three beat, three beat, two beat, in parody of Housman. Both the inner and the outer verses are marked by independent rhyme schemes, each with one verse which is blank to its own scheme but not to the other's.

Of your companionship you think me avid?   1
Remember five o'clock in my christened house   2
while I was reading you the *Song to David*   1
the shadow of a bird ran like a mouse   2
across the floor; and suddenly each wondered   3
when our quick friendship would be quickly sundered. 3

Our selves implore, caught in Christ's hell-embrace: 4
"Trust in distrust, none achieve alone,   5
be not denied us, distrusting our Grace."   4
If, for us, our unchristened selves atone   5
with intercession, our quadruple strength   6
brings circumstances to annoy us less.   7
Both Virgils, each the other's joyousness   7
we'll live a *Comedy* our lifetimes' length.   6

XXI (10)

the fifth of the inverted sonnets, continues in light tone, excepting only as recollection is less gay than anticipation. Z, separated from Y by insistent distrust and hungry for company, imagines that they will not be parted.

KIN

Indigo and Zodiac with tangent bubbles
to bubbles separate these cherished
arduously discovered you's and me's
who smell of resembled smells no longer
in sleepless nostrils; though, like space-caressing
legs of a compass, the smile of pride
(centrifugal, from inside, out)
configurate immortal me's and you's.

Tenderly ruptured pride alone
builds up barricades of communion
where in many-eyed, unblinking stares
before the milkman clinks his jars
tangent foams of you's and me's collapse and fuse
from outside, in; one sapphire yet conscious spiral.

XXII (11a)

like the next two sonnets *is in free verse with criss-cross sound patterns.* Z,
waking early in the city, thinks of all separated friends and lovers and
falls half asleep abandoning friendship for philanthropic solidarity in
rehearsal for final loss of Self. A development of the transvaluated theme
given out in the Coda of III reconciles the positive and negative
themes.

VENUS AND BACCHUS

Hearts ere of sorrow, now thereafter
find their wherefore; these return
with timeless wine. As all to nothing,
henceforth, are the lives of the passing
faces; and a grape god voice
hums in the earth's twisted spin.

Womb-warm spaces that in unborn
women within women carry birth
within birth (as mirror from mirror
carries naught to its internal end)
come, bear interior, infable
rhymes of minds, and cymbals sounding
for iliac dances, through progressive
loves, perplexed by water turning
millstones that grind no corn.

XXIII (11b)

Though human life be a mere recurrence through women unborn,
living, and dead;—

MINUS

Forgotten lodestone lumps recall
shifted weight. Each to each
they embrace in a man, when a man confront
one of many youths. He, or some other,
might now have been that stript joy:
Hungry as lust, immeasurable
all unconceived, all immaternal
immutable, undying and unbounded.

    Our close harmony thought
    resolves to unsaid negative.

XXIV (11 c)

conscious human essence is most conscious in contemplation of divinity,
defined by negatives and understood in silence.

SPIDER

"While that spider Sun drops down her web of sky   1
viol phrases of the bridges are resounding . . ."   2
"Their staccato street lamp notes are pitched too high   1
to reach our ears with their crescendent sounding . . ."   2

  "Why do we labor to make metaphors?   3
  Debussy, Whistler, and both of us are bores . . ."   3
  "In your hair, also is a Hokusai!"   1

XXV (12)

with the second minor turn of the Sequence returns to the scene of XIII and
preserves, though briefly, a light and happy sentiment. The last verse
refers to that Japanese print called "The Wave." *The final repetition of
the first rhyme* reminds the reader that through the course of this dialogue
the spider is dropping to its prey.

PARTING IN HARLEM

Zulu Booze.
In nigger dancing joints'
strawberry ice cream soda light
cigarette butts glow color of ashes.

Bugaboos.
And you'd ring me up to get me up
to make . . . chug-chug . . . the One o'Clock;
but no bell rang.

Baby shoes
now chime with tin-slap tin-slap
tin-slap taxi chains threading the Elevated's
vineless arbor. The telephone burst
its bed table to bloom a black narcissus.
But no bell rang . . . *Voodoos.*

XXVI (13a)

Z wakes up in Manhattan spring noon to the fact that trivial faithless-
ness in Y indicates deeper indifference.

VILLAGE HANGOVER

Stuttering chirrups wake me, fluttering
over the counterpane your cascaded
shadow cast on dream new wine and seltz.
The sun slipped on a skyscraper.
Yellow is turned ash color.
That's Madagascar Blues.
More and more, form shows by shade
till life is lit by faded dream
and, *Zulu Booze*
        and, *Bugaboos*
                and, *Baby shoes.*
Voodoos.
    That's
        Madagas-
           car Blues.

XXVII (13 b)

by recording a dream-waking, recalls the theme of V. The bird that
wakes Z is, like the shadow bird in XXI, a symbol of the transitory.

GET-AWAY

Bounteous Creation! Baking soda cures headaches;
birds could breed without their song-dyed breasts.
Chirrup at my necktie stirrup *My reflection waits for me*
pecks gilt gesso horns of plenty never pecked away.
O bird-type of Good Intention. O Self immortally
alive in act—not act of whetting beak or appetite—but act inane
—(catch thumb in thumb and finger *Sugar's sweet; so is he*
as thumb protrudes through finger and thumb)—
in pure act and Hell of Self Immortal
pure as Hell; or a Sousa March: *The Idiots' Jesus, Forever.*

Bye-bye, Chirrup. *Good-by Forever!* Raven, Bat, and Dove.
Go to bed; light the light; I'll be home late tonight.
Lest you starve in my absence, out the window, Good Intention.
Good-by Forever! Chirrup, bye-bye.

XXVIII (13 c)

farces the positive theme. But to contrast the Immortal Self unfavorably
with Eternal Solidarity is not to deny the Resurrection. Emotional
qualities of religious doctrine are more important than rational qualities.
To recover the emotions and acts originally conveyed through the
doctrine of the Resurrection, reject Immortality. In its current form, it
amounts to a desire for Hell. Oblivion of Self conveys now-a-days
membership in the Body of Christ.

Z gives Y's good intention liberty to the absolute freedom of Hell.

PHALLUS

Friends need not guard each other as a jealous   1
Moslem must segregate his odalisque,   2
no more than one need see the symboled phallus   1
while meditating at an obelisk.   2
    If we could be together day after day,   3
    companionship, pointed with entering wedge   4
    compact, whittled by common task and play   3
    inevitable and slow, would split the pledge   4
    which kisses tallied once in valediction: 5
    that our hidden selves in separation meet.   6
    The corollary's simple contradiction   5
    May render yet the contract obsolete.   6
Habit is evil,—all habit, even speech;   7
and promises prefigure their own breach.   7

XXIX (14)

argues against doubt and distrust in company and separation. *The Shakesperian scheme with its couplet* looks to the fulfillment of the prophecy made to Cain at Abel's funeral in V.

MIRROR

Had you less charm, our friendship were less frail;   1
were you less young, your charm were more robust.   2
Friendship were frailer did not love entail   1
a loyalty engendered of distrust.   2

Oh I could hate you more than Cain his brother   3
(for friendship is no passion and all zeal,—   4
a jealous ardor for ingenuousness)   5
if we should link our arms one with the other   3
only these arms to find our friendship weak   6
and we no more entitled to their caress.   5

I would not argue with you. I would feel   4
(though God made every other soul unique)   6
a silent scorn for your soul, as the lone   7
too faithful mirrored image of mine own.   7

XXX (14b)

turns from distrust of self and distrust of another to hatred of each
other and of self alike. *Rhymes 4 and 6 are built upon the same sad vowel.*

95

KEEPER

Bragging of hatred, hurling termite threats and   1
Lonely for you, long absent, I invite   2
Agony, having thought unkindly of you.   1
Daggers of blunt chagrin assail me, till I   1
Own to your remembered wyrd, I prize not   2
Only your attributes, but your own essence.   2

None but a God can be his brother's keeper.   3
Undiscerning meddler, mislearned in kindness,   3
Fitter for sensibility, not love, were   4
One who would pine to hem your heart in his heart.   3
Wittingly I would never feel thus for you.   4
Pity is kin to scorn, but far more cruel.   4
Quit now of friendship we can never be.   4
Sundered our hearts, but never more our minds.   3

XXXI (14c)

the eighth inverted sonnet rhymed at the beginnings not the ends of the verses,
sinks into recognition of the fact that friendship can continue only at the
price of separation.

POLITICAL SELF-PORTRAIT
1919-1939

*To them
whose names are
anonymous
but whose deeds
immortal*

ACKNOWLEDGEMENTS

EARLIER versions of these numbers appeared in *Alcestis; Anathema; Arise; Banners of Brotherhood; Bozart-Westminster; Compass; Exile Anthology; Furioso; Hinterland; Modern Monthly; New Democracy; New Directions 1939; Partisan Review; Poetry; A Magazine of Verse; Sewanee Review; Triad Anthology; Vanguard Verse, Poems for a Dime.*

They have benefited from readings provided by Boston University, Dartmouth, Harvard, and Tufts Colleges; the Adult Education Center, Capitoline Cooperative Homebuilders; Community Youth, the League Against War and Fascism, the Council of Christians and Jews (all of Boston); the Chelsea Labor Lyceum; the Cambridge Poetry Forum; the Poetry Societies of New England and America (that is to say, of New York City); WIXAL and other Radio Broadcasting Stations; units of the Socialist and of the Socialist Workers Parties; the Young People's Socialist League of Boston, Fitchburg and New Bedford; the Workmen's Circle in Ashland, Dorchester and Worcester; and a WPA Writers' Group of Lynn.

They have benefited no more from the "Bards" and other hearings by fellow poets, of whom S. Foster Damon was chief; and from patient, alert secretaries like Marjorie Lauder, James Kergis, Marion Code, and Kenneth Porter, the poet and scholar.

The author regrets that such references as those to Kronstadt and to "Red Fascism" pass beyond poetic license towards political license; but is unable to find apter language.

THE WORD IS DEED

FOR KENNETH BURKE

John begins like *Genesis*:
In the Beginning was the Word;
Engels misread: *Was the Deed.*
But, before ever any Deed came
the sound of the last of the Deed, coming
came with the coming Word
(which answers everything with dancing).

In our Beginning our Word:
'Make a tool to make a tool'
distinguished Man from Brute.
(Men who dance know what was done.)
Good and Evil took root
in this, the cause of Destinies
whence every Revolution rose and stirred.

Jubal Cain and Tubal Cain
made the plow and jubilee
to protest, in ranks hostile to Seth
Seth's all-too-loyal mutiny.

Ways to work determinate
moulds for intelligence.
Discoveries follow thence
obscured by fallibilities'
compensating philosophies
doubted soon as heard.
(Who dance not know not what they do.)

But when, against Fate, error wards:
"Frustrate while ye mirror kind
Disaster, blind
Chance, enemies at once and guards . . ."
muscles of thought comply:
"Think, act in answer to desire;
from the will springs Promethean fire."

Deeds make us. May, therefore, when our Last
Judgment find our work be just:
all tools, from foot rules to flutes
praise us; and our deeds' praise find
the Second Coming of the Word.
(Dance, each whose nature is to dance;
dance all, for each would dare the tune.)

SOME PLANS ARE SIMPLE

FOR THOMAS EMERSON PROCTOR II

When Alexander 'd conquered Egypt's Land
he marched his armies to a wall of air
that lensed impregnable, the South. His troops deployed.
In their midst rose the suppliant Conqueror:
"Ranges of Eden! Fragrant River-Spring!
every maneuver centered on your sack.
We long to seed whole Provinces with your grasses;
to lavish all people with your bake and brew.
They, knowing no hunger, then would do no more evil;
I am hungering for the hungering," the Deliverer cried:
"Open, you door!" No door opened.

But a scout who ran up to the General chariot
led to a moat's brink, where Eden's reaching
waters rested; and carp, all striped with gold
slipped between ferns and the reflected myrrh.
The scout reported: "These smell like frankincence
when washed and grilled." Scooping cat-quick, Alexander
caught one: "You Bird, you! Sing with winging fins;—
your coined teeth glint like tribute . . ." But the fish grinned
and slithered off, safe, under a watercress.
"Must Eden shun me in all living forms?
Open the door," he begged. No door opened.

But from East and West its walled-out women busied
to lay an argent board with delicate spun silver

From querulous guts; in conquerors' courtesy
he queried, "Can we eat bullion?" But the queen demanded:
"Is there no bread in your country? Must you go
with your young troopers, trampling our young grain?"
"I am a madman, come near to the world's end
to be instructed with old-woman mockery.
Open, inpenetrable air! Open me
one single token to carry in my triumph
that my Vanquished may know their vanquished Victor."
(Jesus, also, wept.)

No door opened. Over the air rampart
tossed (with short wind and dust) a skull
bounded, and ran, and rolled to him, lisping:
"I know nothing, but once from Eden come
desire proof . . ." Alexander picked it up
caressed and (puzzled) cupped it in one sad fist
of his just balance which had scaled tribute
from the unsealed and emptied treasuries of the world.
The skull weighed down all the silver from the table.
"Open this oracle," commanded the Commander.

"You know . . . the Eye . . . you know, the . . ." "I know nothing
but once to Eden come, desire proof."
"Pinch a little dust . . . Powder the socket . . . See, the pan
rises . . . ever so slightly; ever so slightly . . . Ever so,—
the Eye, insatiable as oblivion."
He grasped those lobeless ears. The Macedonian
lips caressing that lipless (loveless) mouth
murmured, "You measure of Hell; you plumb of the Abysm."
And the whole skull resounded back the murmur;
"You measure of Hell; you plumb of the Abysm."
He gazed down, deep, at sightless depth;
and wept; . . . No door in all that wall of air.

TWO TONGUES IN A TOWER

FOR HAROLD LOEB

Back in the iron tower he said, "When I left the tower
the ground shook under foot." "Did the ground-swell shake
any more," she wondered, "than my legs trembled under me?
What had we, then, to fear but nerves teased by a wind?"
"Was it a wind or the earthquake?" he asked; "Do not open the window.
Unroll the graph. Plot curves. Compare; predict;
record; I have given the numbers." But her eyes, which proved his numbers
filled with tears as she heard the wet of the night ask:
'Were there voices calling?' Yes, voices of thin fear,
sigh for calm, soaring tall to the iron, grim tower:

"This spent of calm is not the calm we want.
Half our dread is lest the tower fall in flood
or fissure." "How *can* you continue your figures?" she asks. "Or *you*,
your tears?" he answers, and quietly placing the casement *against*
the wind, calls out his report: "It is not the flood; but more
drought and wind. Not yet the earthquake," he says clearly,
"but a wind!" and locks the window. She: "They hear the wind,
Statistician, give them statistics." And he? "They ask for bread."
He has lost the key to the larder. The lid of the bread box
is too thickset for tack hammers. He will go on charting predictions.

But the tongued wings' eleventh hour broadcast
they must answer. Too soon now, mutinous and stern
mariners'll come with skeleton key and sledges, abrupt
on this tower to open the larder or with key and oil or with hammers . . .
"To give longshoremen a handout of dry loaves
and salt fish?" he will ask. "Yes. Fish, large
as loaves; loaves, large as baskets," she will answer.
"Shall weepers be fed also?" he'll wonder, as she'll wonder:
"Shall I have, then, more sufficient company of love,"
as when he said (half aloud) to himself; "*Hear that storm.*"

CAIN AND SETH

FOR POWERS HAPGOOD

Warrior-Masons of *our* City of Seth invest
their City of Cain. Though shapely armoured wings
glide death over, your tunnels worm their walls.
But within perpetual riot, will friend know friend?

Their tell-tale countersigns tell foe of foe
while deeds distinguish secret citizens
of Seth in Cain and Cain in Seth, but what
of neutrals who'd command the tone of soldiers
only to melt into a mist of birches?

These are they who scatter confusion in council
and give us trembles like a woman's birth pangs.
Along the streets of Seth they walk with guilty
Judas eyes (blue lamps); and, spreading glooms
on gallants, spend atlas bones to water.

LANTERNS OF TIME

FOR KENNETH PATCHEN

While evening darkens, though the East mock dawn;
air cool stone, sea-cold of stone, stone
blood-fevered lie where burning brush and jetsam
(yet smouldering while turning tide lappings yet
tap them) were scarlet upon azured sulphurous air.
Dark earth and magnet West against the magnet
East contract before the impacting sky
gathers to itself all flax-coloured below
ascendant Mars and, waning, the sickle Moon.

... Power by owning without making, *theirs*;
hunger, ignorance, disease, and war
then *ours* forever pleasure to make all own

107

instantly (purple whirlpool) instantly
(heed as we may unrealizable hope,
wealth, wisdom, health, and peace)
whirlpools turn the rings of their speed-darkened steel . . .

Easterly upon Wheelwright project
(diaphonous, nimbused)
dead Doctors of Emancipations past;
who, like voices calling over water,
when they are far, seem near.
Westwardly Wheelwright projects
(darker than deepening cloud)
live Martyrs to Emancipations
which, when they are near, seem far.

A moon and star reflect a star and the Moon
below that shadow of a fence along the fencing shadow
pile-green drawbridge across Lobster Cove.
Here (on this abandoned wharf, long heaped
of granite chip by fishermen, schooned under)
none note the wolves' rib-stare that looks
out at us ready to eat you up . . .

It seems a Venice (tourist-viewed)—some Delft
depicted in Victorian tempera.
Shift focus; see the bonfire Naples' mountain
where Vulcan works (boss of his open shop)
friend with no man whom no bosses befriended
unprisoned; but by servile freedom bound
in fitter bonds than his, that bind the Titan lad,
Prometheus, to dead, deadening dominion.

"Wheels" flashes light from a sharpened scythe in lithe
light from the moon-sickle, flashing in the sky.
A Finn mallets his spike to split a granite stone.
Thunder is pounded in dry thunder clouds.

From instant West with embers and starred Moon,
turn to the past persistent evening of the day

whose close burns lighter than the start.
Face lingered, eastern, lumined afterglow's
serene (no, smug) content with sated good.
Let's look at grandpa's chromolithographic
stereopticon views: The Paris Salon, 1888;
or try the mother-of-pearl music box;
and then, Brahms on the Radio.

. . . How fleshly is stone's warmth. How terrible were
mammals like the Moving Rock; or a vegetable
turning carnivorous to shed about wild
strawberries and gooseberries and the sweet single rose
itching chevron fluff of Stalin's Red Fascism.

Long before all known cause for every evil known
will melt in neighborwealth and commonworld;
shall men and maelstrom men stir unknown hatred
when hatred between class can move men's wills no more?
The matrix of our vulcanic power has boiled
forth more peasant greed than greed for coin.
Shall our too philanthropic combat gender
from dogma-wickedness yet unborn
such war as even God could never fight?

Now swathed in swastika'd caparisons
over their cancered bellies that digest their tripes
horses march in lathered blood up to their nostrils.
Here, where there be no men, need "Wheels" be a man?
Take warning from Israel's unrealizable
hope (and losing lazy faith of busy
innocence) heed stiff Rabbinic queries:
How do fools fear sin? Can the shy learn?
Even a blind hen finds sometimes a good corn.
But how to bring others to the good, who are not so ourselves?

. . . Ears trained to Epic in the crudest News
are deaf; corporate lips once purged with coal
tongued from blood-quenched braziers of wage war
are dumb to answer such deaf tittle-tattle.

Kronstadt, victorious over Petersburg
Kronstadt, vanquished by Leningrad
has simply got to try again;—
and soon, with scoop of international glee
microphones divulgate phalanxes
to-day-after-tomorrow's news:
City of Cain Hands Up To Seth . . .

Sing, therefore; hammer thought-rhymes ring and jingle
again upon their factual anvil.
Smithies of necessary morals weld
our single broken sword. We shall command
the hands behind their guns; and brains behind the hands
mate the serpent sword to flaming guns.

PECCATUM ORIGINALE

FOR HAROLD LASKI

Original Sin (compassionate catechism)
made errors in history seem geometric, like
the sombre bank of verdure, bank of cloud
which lakes this clear East of sky, these sky-clear waters
here even clearer than reflected moon and starlit
star-shaken dreamlight which shook under
seeming-actual Holy Roman Empire
whose fear (history-book prefigured) of our doom
still wars against the unrealizable hope
that sated sovereignty can famish avarice.

In a City, built on seven-mounded virtue
where Adam's sons guard his oracular bones
Augustin enkeeped standards of deep desire
by which Seth'd measure Cain's accomplishment.
But making the Christ a Gracchus not a Spartacus
this will wherein a hundred minds have dwelt
imprisoned lost rebellion in word mazes
and, welding revolt to worldly acquiescence,

let both rival tyrants, Pope and Emperor
(brigand with brigand contending for dominion
like *anti*-Christ with anti-*Christ* contending)
dismiss hostile sowers on rival sowing
of acquiescent tares and of resistant thistles.

And by his City of God, the African Doctor
(prime to perform the funereal piety
of writing his soul's sole life; Utopia's
Pious Aeneas, with Plato for Anchises)
swerved Dante from his highroad, made him wander
toward Cain always in long trek for Seth.
For Dante would have lit with lamps of peace and praise
Augustin's tocsin-towered double dome,
in life a cave; in death a lamp to poets and doctors.
With irresponsibility, supernal
as wrestling weather giants overhead
he'd choose the Emperor (who should govern fact)
as governor of truth as well, because the Pope
(sole proper servitor of truth) served lies.
He'd wield the disciples' swords of Word and Deed
against the Petrine Standard of the Keys
but for august Imperial discipline
whose unsure building founded sure fall . . .

The throbbing East, that once so luminous,
limned the lit windows underneath, now dims
like Dante, fed with a hundred ages' oil,—
once rebel in spirit, now Judas to rebellion
his star lamp shrilling like the day-star fallen
to an old moat water where waterlilies pout. . .

More sad than lost and unrecoverable loves
prophecies grow feckless because half-fulfilled.
Turn, turn unperturbably, turn West.
Pity would-be patchers of Roman liberty
who, fed with laborers' word-giving bread
do not give back bread-giving words to men.
They're, all of them, dull to drumming wings in desert

III

caves where prophets gather answers against kings
and whither opinionated wills retreat, to woo
the advance of freedom's phoenix paraclete
whose ashen flaming throat cries, "Yes!" cries, "No!"

When such turn rebel they would lust to wreathe
Lucifer with acorn and oakleaf
snatched from Jesus, Proletarian archrebel
(birth-star, faded, like fallen Lucifer's day-star).
Such (whether acquiescent or resistant) alway
plead: "Christ does not cause the fall of Rome.
That Miscreant who from Heaven fell, fells Caesar."
Such will plead such when socialized Babylon
must give beneath them to let catacomb
anarchia to breadth of breath and light,
and the Boys open from graves of duty upon power's
last (and I mean last) domesday to their habitual joys.

ANATHEMA. MARANATHA!

FOR MURIEL RUKEYSER

Oh for that rose of Bolshevism which holds
memory of its own budding,—and not this;—
this drooping prophecy of wormed potpourri,
Moscow's abomination of desolation;—
zig-zag marshlight of illth,
too "practical" five year planner of,—defeat;—
up-start Pope fanned by peacock lies:
"Were we ever wrong? No. We were never wrong.
We offer no resistance to Fascism.
We were correct before, during, and after.
What we could not do, Nazism has done.
We have committed no mistakes."

Infallible dunce, ineffably vincible,
we'll burn your cancer to a root in us.
As our waxing forces upon nature wax

force in ourselves, our forces over others wane,
and though your lamp'll never out, it fades ...
fades before searchlight material humane.

Flivvers herd fireflies down the sumac slope;
the trees stir; the tides turn; the cloud
theater-curtain closes across the Moon;
and a landward sea wind lifts over the lawn,
with dancing leaves, the tilth that Spring thaws lent the brine;
while (to a Westland gale and heat lightnings
a-rumble over Coffin's Beach, laden
with hay scent of storm) the flotsam rubbish pile
bursts once more into flame. Flame doubled now
where late were the acid Moon and one star mirrored.
The tempest's cribbed abundance bursts its bin;
plum trees drop worm-soft fruit and ratted bark.
Thunder begins the night. In three days, it may clear.
The stars will bud.

COLLECTIVE COLLECT

FOR ARCHIBALD MACLEISH

Jump, Jesus! Jump. Up, do not stand for it.
Take the snake-wand of the quick-turnover
Thief-God from the hands of fortunate would-be
Caesars of Wall Street,—each with a pickled egg
face kept in that cut glass bar room brine
—the painless, premature martyrdom
of weakend family men,—before whom sprawled
(to paraphrase their appropriate laureate)
in a stream-lined, though bespattered, underthing
Columbia lies on her belly, her flank yellow.

You, Joshua, whose forearm with Creator biceps
fans the wind of freezing ghostly rage
(while boom the double guns of Word and Deed)
you, Christ, whose winding wrist with Fortune's sinews
span burning whip-cords athwart money-changers;

wash the curse of Mercury from coo-coo
clock doorways of the in-and-outers;
remove from middle poets-by-will the shrined
lackey god of households who would cry:
"In Hoc Signo Vinces" to the Caduceus
Dollar Sign ($) anti-Crucifix.
Jump, Jesus! Quick, Christ, up! Do not stand for it!

RESURGE FROM DECRESCENCE

FOR SHERRY MANGAN

M." woke to Mangan's room in Lynn, and hears
the April roll to Long Beach from Marblehead;
and a light truck bump; and the eggbeater
inside its radiator churn salt air
all the way to the brownstone Town Hall:
"Why did Jack call Jesus the Ur-Rebel?
I understand that Lucifer is Rebel."
       Waves in nines scoot up the tawny shore
through kelp, against a punge of Spring-burned
leaves, and Mangan answers her: "Wheels said
at the Indian Summer time of yesterday:
'Lucifer is arch-Rebel in the Rebellion
of Rebels who rebel but for Dominion.' "

Five cars making the slope purr, like stalking
cats, past the window's oval oculus;
and drawing mingled roar of four waves with them
toward that Common, shaped like Magog's boot print;
scatter the carrier pigeon croon
over torn-down factories to dumped brackish marshes:
"Wheelwright's a Protestant; doesn't he 'like' Luther?"
       "When on February's summer day we flivvered
along where Nahant looks on Neponset's
Blue Hill dolphins dive into Boston Bay.
Wheels said: 'That timid heresiarch, admonishing hayseeds:
All *Power* is of God to reverence

Dynasts as Demigods, forged (on the palimpsest
of Paul's License to Natural Right):
All Power is of God
Decretals of Divine Right of Kings.' "

"Then what does Puritan Wheelwright make of Calvin?"
Six waves lie fallen on Lynn's threshold, and the
seventh saucers the flat parabola;
John Joseph Sherry Mangan testifies:
"Calvin, to be august, was Augustinian.
(This showy pun reveals Wheels' ignorance.)
But braggart slaves (through centuries' unceasing
ever-lessening reverberation
between antiphonate silences)
proclaim his State pastor of unfed sheep."
    "A would-be rebel prince by principle,
then what does Wheelwright make of Machiavelli?"
"Old Nick quoted with sound of tongueless mountains
and words under torture as false as deeds of princes
the net cost of power to all rising classes."
"Shall Lucifer, then, clang when Kingdom fall
in fall of every state where every boss is king?"
Waves in nines curl kelp in the sulphured cove
and still (with three's in three's) recede to slow, purple tide.

BREAD-WORD GIVER

FOR JOHN, UNBORN

John, founder of towns,—dweller in none;
Wheelwright, schismatic,—schismatic from schismatics;
friend of great men whom these great feared greatly;
Saint, whose name and business I bear with me;
rebel New England's rebel against dominion;
who made bread-giving words for bread makers;
whose blood floods me with purgatorial fire;
I, and my unliving son, adjure you:
keep us alive with your ghostly disputation

make our renunciation of dominion
mark not the escape, but the permanent of rebellion.

Speak! immigrant ancestor in blood; brain
ancestor of all immigrants I like. Speak,
who unsealed sealed wells with a flame and sword:
  'The springs that we dug clean must be kept flowing.
  If Philistines choke wells with dirt,—open
  'em up clear. And we have a flaming flare
  whose light is the flare that flames up in the people.

  'The way we take (who will not fire and water
  taken away) is this: prepare to fight. If we
  fight not for fear in the night, we shall be surprised.
  Wherever we live, who want present abundance
  take care to show ourselves brave. If *we* do not try
  they prevail. Come out,—get ready for war;
  stalwart men, out and fight. Cursed
  are all who'll come not against strong wrong.
  First steel your swordarm and first sword.
  But the second way to go? and deed to do?

  'That is this: Take hold upon our foes and kill.
  We are they whose power underneath a nation
  breaks it in bits as shivered by iron bars.
  What iron bars are these but working wills?
  Toothed as spiked threshing flails we beat
  hills into chaff. Wherefore, handle our second
  swords with awe. They are two-edged. They cut their
             wielders' hearts.'

FISHERMAN

FOR LLOYD COLLINS

On this Atlantic shore
between the Swallow Cave
and Spouting Horn,
the tall, vulcanic Pulpit Rock
with pendant kelp is veiled

116

by drying fish nets.
Such were the offerings to the Sea Priapus
of a Piraean fisher,
who, in reflections of his god,
between a star fish
and a swimming star
saw his own face reflected.

CHELSEA EXCHANGE

FOR JOHN PEALE BISHOP

Between the double sundial of two towers
the Woolworth Building and the Empire State
(five-and-ten cathedral in baked lace;
efficient dog-house for bitched Smiths)

lies an Arcadia of steel, concrete, and grime
whose shepherds sleep on shelves reached up stepladders
perfumed with musk of immemorial urine,
powdered with dust that daylight never sees.

Here Centaurs trot,—half men, half reputations;—
martyrs to "living," fooled by the feel of life.
They would revisit the Sundays of their promise
before they turned all-right-Nick, up-town thinkers.

Half-arsed martyrs to the feel of thinking,
Thracians, late of adolescent fermentation,
less was their promise broken than the spell
of half-formed thoughts put in three-quarter words.

Do not, rheumatic Centaurs (while your nymphs
preserve in alcohol schoolgirl complexions)
print drink-plus conversation to restate
three-quarter thought in hangover, the doom

of citied Thracians, not (like their wine-god) twice born.
Your words, sobered, turn blackboard diagrams,

never to work the oracular change to deed.
Centaurs abandoned! Nymphs who attend Cassandra!

SEVEN FROM FOUR

FOR SPENCE BURTON

Cain's men by seven sacraments
obliterate their memories of deeds'
collective guilt by separate penitence
for virtue's seven-fold shadow-sin.
But men of Seth make the four elements
(which are Eternity's porphyrogen
inheritors: Water; Air; Fire; Earth)
serve conscious will's oracular instruments
through outward signs of python spiralled power.

Fourfold anointed in these elements
washed in the font of burning light,—our faith
(regenerate in doubt's second innocence;
as seed flourish though flowers no longer flower)
thus implemented, can possess seven
hale potencies. Confirmed from impotence
the cube bursts; its pyramids, cloven
release their elemental forces; and this first:

how thought's pre-sacrament (primordial
truth's untiring mill wheel) burning
water to thirst, oceans to vapor, churn
actuals with purpureal wish. That was the first
step of our process from ambivalence.
And this the second:—how from air's ordinal
and azure love in anger's smouldering urn
our memories fodder the winged stallion.

That was the second. Third:—how genital
torches of scarlet liberty's penance confessional
(corrupted more in church than market place;
less on hearth than hassock, or by forge than deathbed)

burn justice to ash. And this encyclical
third teaches at last:—how vegetative grace
(diurnal celebrant, with scythe and horn
of harvest flax planted and harvested)
dispense thanksgiving, grapes and corn
nuptial for the living, unction for the dead.

TITANIC LITANY

FOR LEON TROTSKY

Prometheus!
Prototypal Christ, pre-crucified
pushing the invisible
advance upon our pushes upon chaos.
Discoverer and inventor, never let 'em say:
"Human nature cannot change."
Institutor of fire's Sacrament
and outward forms of conscious inner will;
Prometheus!
Forethought of freedom (freedom
for her and him; concrete, in that and this)
Titan, tortured by the tyrant vulture
whom Vulcan riveted as firmly as machines
can rivet laborers to capital;
Prometheus!
O, let it never be said that the human of nature cannot
change. Saul changed to Paul. All saints change
man's nature, as men change nature's change.
Show us in our own acts that we hear our supplication.
Never a Saint is revered who was not reviled
as a rebel. Every rebel, in so far prophet
breeds holy doubt and skeptic faith in deeds'
Melchizedekian Succession.
While boom the double guns of Act and Word,
mutating fire swims through the protestant
blood of Christ, erect above your shadowed rock
Prometheus!
Our supine Crucifixion.

FOOTSTEPS

FOR THE YPSLS

CHORUS

stamping with increasing speed

FOOTSTEPS.

Drumbeat	beat	[drum
beat drumbeat		
drum	beat	
Drumbeat Drumbeat		
Drum	Beat Time	
TiRa		

[horn
[stamping

FIRST SEMI-CHORUS

led by LABOR LAWYER *and* EAGLE

Money talks. In Good Times
beware. It says, "Save your Dimes.
Spend here to save. Save to spend.
Lend to borrow. Borrow to lend."

CHORUS

Spend faster. Faster, nearer, faster.

[silence

FIRST SEMI-CHORUS

The Wage-Profit System, fecund
with Surplus Value every second
for centuries, has NOT been weakened.
Behold! And
though the Golden Age of Europe pass,
Gold Sand
as through an Hour Glass
shall flow through the Americas:—

EAGLE

while yearning Social Research flowers
with Co-operative Cauliflowers
grown in rows with the yellow Sun
Flowers of Company Unison.

[horn

120

CHORUS

TiRa, blow-blow, TiRa!

[*stamping*

TWO EAGLES

Recovery can never end
for, the Bad Times Profit brings,
make small savers spend
their savings.
Watch your step. Show some pep.
Hold your job.

CHORUS

! TiRa !

[*stamping, horn*

THREE EAGLES

TiRa! Hoo-Ra-Drum, beat them dumb.
Beat time. Drum, beat.

[*drum*
[*horn*

CHORUS

! Ti-Ra !

TWO, THREE EAGLES

Will you
meet the Problem of To-day?
You share your work. We pare your pay.
Coca-Cola keeps you keyed up.
You must not let the Speed-Up
kill you.
Live to see Recovery reach higher stages
with shorter Hours, but for lower Wages.

[*horn*

CHORUS

TiRa-HooRa. Hou-Ray . . .

[*stamping*

BOY, *raising arm*

I'm a Man, not a Machine.

LAWYER

You talk like an Anarchist.

THREE EAGLES

Learn to like Taylor Routine
or be scrapt. You're worn and lean

121

anyhow. Take your Check.
Stop. Hold your job. Drum. Show some Pep.   [*drum*

SECOND SEMI-CHORUS OF WORKERS
Footsteps. Foot-*beats*. Watch *your* Step.   [*stamping*

GIRL, *raising arm*
My hand is mangled at the wrist.

LAWYER
Now you talk Syndicalist.

SECOND EAGLE
Get out! Quick, you Bolshevik!
We have no room, here, for the sick.
                                              [*muffled drum*

SECOND SEMI-CHORUS
Drum! Beat nearer, nearer.

CHORUS
Beat Time! Drum, beat again.
Ti-Ra. HooRay. Speed up, beat Time, Speed, Time!
Speed Up, beat Time. Speed, Time!

EAGLE
Drum up more trade. Fire less men.
Get out, 15! You're fired, 10!

FIRST SEMI-CHORUS
! TiRa !
                                              [*stamping*

WORKER
We, the foundation stones of crazed Humanity . . .

TWO WORKERS
Weavers whose nature is to weave . . .

THREE WORKERS
We, Laborers, with the keys to unlock locked-up Industry,
long find our natural right to live
the prey of that same legal Robbery
which starved Grandfather's Husbandry
and now plows under food while our Wives starve.

SECOND SEMI-CHORUS, *with raised arms*
Is there no Butcher's Axe to cleave
from shoulder-bones of Tyranny
hid heads of open Banditry?

BOY
Workers,
with nothing to lose . . .

FIRST SEMI-CHORUS
but your brains . . .

Shirkers . . .
pay your Poll Tax . . .
don't be dense . . .
show some sense . . .
go home when it rains . . .
RELAX!

LAWYER, *with night stick*
Move along. Shove along.

GIRL
FOOTSTEPS, AWAKE!   [*tramping*

LAWYER
Streets are free. Take your time.
Why worry?
Softly, slow. Keep off the Grass.
What's your hurry?
Let Trouble wait. Make Time slowly.

BOY
DUMB, AWAKE! BEAT TIME!   [*tramping*

GIRL
who, stripped to her red shirt, has mounted a soapbox
These Red Pamphlets, here, the Free
Literature of Misery
champion Humanity.

LAWYER, *snatching*
?They do? Let's see . . .

123

RED GIRL

Bosses, beware
the war you would prepare
lest your conscripts declare
War on the War-Maker.

LAWYER, *snatching*

This must mean Mutiny.
What have we here?

BOY

who, stripped to his red shirt, has mounted a soapbox

Expropriate the Profiteer!
Right is Might. Unite to fight!
Exterminate the Parasite!

LAWYER, *reading and scratching his ear*

This, to me,
seems disrespect for Property!   [*laughter*

RED BOY, *punctuating with clenched fist*

Wash the stale sweat from your backs,
hang-dog Proletariat!
Repudiate demands
of the Emperors of Bets, Finance
Rents, Interests, Percents.
Toilers, toil for him who toils.
Unite your fights for Mills and Farms.
To the Victor be the spoils.
Abandon jealous stealth.
Debt-Autocrats now dominate
dry-rotting Agrarian Democrats.
No State can stand, half slave, half free.
The Franchise of Wage Slavery
commands Industrial Commonwealth.

RED GIRL, *with hand to mouth*

Exterminate the Parasites!
Sound the alarums,—
attack!

[stamping, as part of the SECOND SEMI-CHORUS *strip
to red shirts and stand ready to attack, but the greater
part drift to the* FIRST CHORUS

LAWYER

! Why! Is this Treason?
Read it louder

RED GIRL, *with both hands to mouth*
EXTERMINATE THE PARASITES!
EXPROPRIATE THE EXPROPRIATORS!

LAWYER, *to* FIRST SEMI-CHORUS
Treason! Shout "treason."
Reds are Traitors!

FIRST SEMI-CHORUS
!TREASON! TRAITORS!

LAWYER *to* RED GIRL
Does the Traitress dare yell louder?

RED GIRL, *with arms outstretched*
!EXPROPRIATE THE EXPROPRIATORS!
!DESOLATE THE DESOLATORS!

LAWYER, *to* FIRST SEMI-CHORUS
Beat both Reds into a chowder
in the Name of Law and Order.

RED BOY
What you call "Order," "Common Sense" and "Law"
is known as Anarchy, before
our tribunals of Common Sense.
We commit the ancient crime
for human justice in our time
whose Conscience is our recompense.
Empires of your intellect
builded on ruin, shall be wrecked
by spies against spy, and ever more
conspirators against conspirator.
Dominion, with the brain in league
against our hearts' and wills' intrigue

rising from nothing, falls thence
conspired against by all intelligence.

WORKINGMEN, *who have joined the* FIRST SEMI-CHORUS

Dumbbell, Dumbbell! one more victim.
First we club him, then convict him.   [*stamping*

    WORKINGWOMEN, *who have joined*

Make her come clean!   [RED BOY *and* GIRL *fall*
Bathe her in a shower-bath of burning
gasoline!

    MEN AND WOMEN

Ship them cold across the Border
in the Name of Law and chowder!
They had no right to fight for bread.
There is no right to strike. Instead: [*horns*

    CHORUS

Char him in iron chains;
with faggots pitched in tar
till his bones' chain remains
a spoil of Order's War.
Blow, blow TiRa!   [*silence*

    Remaining SECOND SEMI-CHORUS

Red Front, march on!
Red Girl, Red Boy are gone.
We mourn them only thus:
Red Front! March on!
Many anonymous
leaders have gone before;
RED FRONT! MARCH ON!
Lest comradeship and valor fade,
we make *this* in our War on War
our abatis and barricade:
EXTERMINATE THE PARASITE.
!EXPROPRIATE THE EXPROPRIATORS!

    LAWYER, *flag-waving*

With Silver Drum, shout "HooRa's"
to the white, spangled stars,

126

while, caged in red and white bars,
the Eagles rage:

EAGLE, *flapping and flopping*

Will common people never understand
the Going-under of the Evening-Land?

TWO EAGLES

The world is heading toward a new Dark Age,

THREE EAGLES

and the Fall of Rome looms just ahead.

WORKER

Your History gives the poor poor place . . .
Your Science stultifies the race . . .

TWO WORKERS

Law lets you robbers get away
with Murder,—High Pay, or Low Pay,—

THREE WORKERS

Where you see Darkness, we see Red
Dawn at last.

more of SECOND CHORUS, *with raised fists*

The Big Turn-Over lies ahead.
The Future overturns the Past.
Proletarian Dictators
from countless capitals of Peace
until Capitalism cease
make war on care-makers.

LAWYER

Take care! Beware!
The Past lives to seed the Present;
and as cackling of startled geese
saved Jupiter Capitoline
startled Capitalism's nine
Judges in plenary conclave . . .

SEMI-CHORUS

Sterile heart! Arid groin!

LAWYER

... unanimously concur to save
Motherhood and Childhood's pleasant
free will and choice against malfeasant
foes of your Life-long Liberty's pursuit
by Property to its secure Grave.
Let all who would these powers enjoin
be mute.

EAGLES, *stripped to black shirts, saluting*

Take care!
Burning Fasces boil
cauldrons of castor oil
to cure acerb rages
against the Robbery of Wages.
Beware!

more of SECOND SEMI-CHORUS *stript to red shirts*

Footsteps wakening, awaken
demonstrating
march, unshaken
unhesitating
and without fear declare:

still more of SECOND SEMI-CHORUS *stript to red shirts*

Make desolate the Desolators!
Vulcanos belch from all their Craters.
Turmoil stirs.
Might is right! Unite
Peacelover with Warriors.

FARMER, WORKER, SOLDIER, SAILOR, *clasping hands*

! Expropriate Expropriators !
Desolate despair.
Create creators'
Commonwealth.
Labor's
Community of Neighbors
bases its bulk on everywhere.

FIRST EAGLE

?Have you no Culture? no Tradition?
?Nor fear of God? Love for Religion?

WORKER, SOLDIER, SAILOR, *pointing*

All are as platitudinous
wicked and pusillanimous
as you, high-browed Eagle,
who made them thus.
Karl Marx has joined Knowledge with Power:
the secrets sought by Saint and Sceptic
are opened to the light in our
Materialistic Dialectic.
Your priests defend hypocrisies.
We despise teachers and priests
who serve as lackeys to your feasts.
Your Gods were always our God's enemies.

LAWYER *and* TWO EAGLES, *with drooping wings*

We have no prayer, but dread;
and no teacher, but fear
that our judgment draw near
which is prepared.
Until your Kingdom come
we pray to you instead:
"Give us your daily bread."
Your dying Leader spared
our fathers when he said:
"They know not what they do."
But our deliberate will has long been done.
Our gory Sacrament
provides us gold from lead,—
from labor, surplus.
As we forgive our debts, may you
forgive
us, when you come against us;
for we would not outlive
our Power and our Glory
when they are spent,—
and dead . . .

FIRST SEMI-CHORUS, *saluting and drawing car*

HooRa! TiRa! Parade. [*horns*

EAGLE *mounting car*

Submit, slum children, to be taught
reverence for Juggernaut.
Beat kettle drums with merriment. [*drum*

FIRST SEMI-CHORUS

HooRay! TiRa! TiRade! [*horn*

TWO EAGLES

We represent the Government
in which your frustrate wills are caught
by this gilt sacrificial car
whose axle bears the Swastika;
and whose Battle Standard intertwines
Ticker Tape with Dollar Signs

FIRST SEMI-CHORUS

!Hooray! TiRa! HooRa! [*horn and drum*

THREE EAGLES

Prepare;
be not surprised:
learn of the democratic mission:
Fascism's imminent
rationalized
fulfillment of frustrate fruition
is mass torture by Inquisition
secularized
to propagate percent percent.

SECOND SEMI-CHORUS, *driving* FIRST SEMI-CHORUS *back*

Drum! beat, Drum. Beat down! [*stamping*
Down, beat down
Fasces and Swastika. [BLACK SHIRTS *fall*
Down, decadent White Collar Classes! [LAWYER *falls*
Down with the State you represent! [EAGLES *fall*
Power to the Masses' [*some white collar workers lay off their*

130

Classless Government!   *coats showing red shirts*
Trumpet the Comedy of Fate.   [*horn*
Hold its ultimate Plebescite.
Beware! The final Revolution stirs!
Beware its strength,—the permanent peacemakers.   [*stamping*
Thunder footbeats drum
under steel skies red torches lit.
Beware! At length
conscripts declare
War on Warmakers.
Permanent Revolution stirs!

        RED BOYS, *fighting*

      Drumbeat
              Drumbeat
                    beat and Rebel cry;
Workers' white fists
        Farmers' brown fists
                Peons' black fists;
Soldiers' cannon
        Sailors' cannon
                boom and doubled
drum.
Drumbeat
    beat and Rebel cry;
Father's pistol; Brother's pitted body; Mother's
step and sister tears (the Baby's broken
drum) young Victim Blood beat, drum;
beat, fighting Blood of vengeance, Blood of victors;
drumming, beaten drum
              beat
                Drumbeat
                  beat;
drum, heart (old beaten, broken drum) beat . . .

We are beating, Workers, we are beating;
O drum, Blood! Comrade and beating heart
Comrade, Victor, Comrade
Victor, Comrade, Victor.

RED GIRLS, *weeping*

Broken hearts, O, beating Blood,
Blood is Victor.
Victors are broken victims of Blood, victor . . .

FIRST SEMI-CHORUS
[*Muffled drums as biers are laid down*

DRUMBEAT! Drumbeat! Drumbeat! Drumbeat!
!beat, drumbeat!
Drumbeat!   Beat
to stumbling footsteps . . .
We who still live on
forget not who have gone.
[*a Girl and a Worker mount soapbox and
clasp hands on the Red Standard*

RED BOYS

Move to joy and peace from grief and war.   [*whistling*
Red Drums and thin
whistles of Farm Rebellion win.
Workmen! perfect the plain
destiny of History's plan;   [*drum*

RED GIRLS

Millhands and Farmhands, manumit,
who heal a spent Earth's mobile health
with sure medicine,—   [*drum*
move on to fun,—
grim scarcity is gone.

RED BOYS

Masses, emancipate,
close the age-long War of Classes.
Freedmen of the World, create
one, wide creators' Commonwealth.
[*silence*

FULL CHORUS
till the horn gives out the Internationale
Rebel whistles
Workers' *footsteps*
Marxian *heartbeats*
Militant *footsteps*

132

Masses' *footsteps*
              Builders' *drumbeats*
Fighters' *heartbeats*
              Victors' *footsteps*
Victors' *heartbeats*
              Fighters' *footsteps*
Builders' *footsteps*
              Workers' *drumbeats*

    !MARXIAN TRUMPET!
      [*Horn . . .*]
    !HORNS OF PLENTY!

COM-U-NASTY PEACE

FOR RICHARD BLACKMUR

Longshoremen, limberjacks, bogus army
hitch-hiking hunger tramp, ropes of sandwich
hand-me-out bread lines; Hooverville
scavengers; dupes of thrift stamp
get-rich-quick insurance policies
could not beat Banker Sam in thirty-two.

The world's brain houses in its chamfered hive
a dynamo whose poles,—the Yah, the Nah,—
manumit still servile hemispheres
to equatorial lull. Now laborers
(can reptile bowels corrode skeletons?)
embalm their wills in a communal swaddling band.
An acquiescent truce for trade in zeros
(defending 'good' Empire from 'bad' Empire)
disclaims to zenith noon saturate exploitation.

Daughters of the American Revolution;
Order of Cincinnati, Tribe of Tammany;
strike-breaking thugs, strong-arm squads; fighting-cock
leathernecks, stool-pigeons; Ku Klux Klan;

133

the R.F.C., the L.R.B.
were not locked out in 1936.

The while silk-shirted negligence command
that convict chains tow commissary barges
through tactical canals toward the next war,
reclined on fetishes, massaged squash players, growing
bald who rent exclusive homes with spoken dread
for torture games of fascist epicenes (and
unspoken dread of next-door-neighbor Jones)
dispatch brief-belted legions of miners down
death-breathing shafts to garner the curded milk of stone.

Our guns are muzzled-loaded for our Naught Five.
In a Forty Eight is bloodshed a blood-letting?
Lamp-oil burned, not heart's blood spilled, wins war.
Victories are gained inside frightened minds.
Battles are won *with* soldiers, not *by* soldiers.
Wrath, not rage, 'll drill our rifle barrels.

Proletarian Aristocrats,
the whole of the world is a teacher. But it's not easy
(while Walking Delegates display their restive Unions'
Masonic watch-fob panoply of class war)
to take all it could give so easily.

Your philanthropic church turns misanthropic;
and only to unpriestly chamberlains
(nor liberal utter-revolutionary snobs
in fascist Romes or Moscow, Berlins or liberal London
who love the people because they love pity;
whose prying agents teach complacent death
to finger prayer in punctual jugulate swoon)
Janicular doors of economic Peace and War'll swing closed.

Rebels whose hearts, breaking, remember:
Fire when we see whites of eyes;—
his wrath is weak, whose rage can crack his heart.
Though in this Thirty Eight our heart be broken

our Forty Eight prepares a rapid Seventy;—
and modest-colored dawn ushers a western rose
through the doors of the house of the double-faced god of the door.

YOU - U. S. - US

FOR JAMES BRADLEY THAYER

O sing the Daisy Chain of grinning Dead Heads,
and come across, you Youwhos, who'll support War.
Come with pansy petals, and a Penny for your thoughts
to a little Sing-Song.

The tin hat of Mars
is passing upside down. Don't let it drop!
Empty your pockets of Coppers, fillings from black molars,
plugs and buttons, protested notes,
Squares and Compasses, Company Scrip.

Weave a Daisy Chain of "Loves me,—Loves me not"
Richman, Poorman, Beggarman, Thief,
Doctor, Lawyer, Indian Chief
All Created Equal, to be Queen
of the Maybe the President Loves Me,—
Loves me not.

For your song to sing for supper,
sing of goods in wrappers
worth powder to blow them straight
from the Bye-and-Bye of Business
to the Grand Old Way, bye-bye.
Blue Bird, bye-bye.

Sing the Daisy Chain of grinning Dead Heads.
Producer to Consumer, from Millyard to Doorstep
string the Idle along. Stick ramrods up them;
dump gunny sacks of gold, panned out from dried blood,
down their closed throats when their jaws fall; and,
lo! behold the hungry,—streamlined Soldiers now.

By why, O why do they swell, and swelling, turn grey
Dead Heads? Sing them
"War is kind of
—kinder than Starvation,"
and they will swing a Daisy
Chain, with a swing-time song
of grinning Dead Heads, Dead Heads.

Rival Industrial Fakirations (who supported
Woodrow Wilson well, who ill-supported you)
support "Forgotten Man" Roosevelt's War
ahead of time, while there is time,
and get Time-and-a-Half Overtime
weaving a chain of dead grins,
chained to chiming Stop-watch Wrist-watch
Time-clocks,—with a Now Stop Rocking the Boat,—
swinging your grinning swing-time Daisy Chain.

White Collar Youwhos, swathed in fair linen,
keep your shirts on. Keep your chins up.
Not a close shave in the carload of you.
Keep your White Collars white. Keep your soft
"Yes" lips stiff with a Will and a Way;
for Roman Collar Youwhos, with pocketcomb and Crucifix
pass the buck to the Red Cross to put gold cheekbones
under tin hats with a same dead grin.
The way of the Cross is War.

Pass the adhesive tape here
where it does more good than rivets.
Do you really think the War is going to be a flop?
Quick, don't let it drop, don't let it sag before
its time. It was going to be such a Sensible
Little War. Stay with us gauze and hand-grenade,
for we are sick of Peace. We are sick of Peace.
We are Sick. Support the War.
Shore it up. Put props under it. Don't
let it drop in the Coming World Community Church Drive
to save the World from becoming

the Coming World Community
Sing-Song.

Don't forget to think hard.
Think hard. Have you thought
how some nonsensical, forgotten Clock'll strike?
Some Whistle let off steam?
Loud speaker Guns speak a strange Tone?
And these Guns shoot the Wrong Way Round?
And Guns and Clock and
shrieking whistle clang one Carrillon?

And the Face of the Clock, looking out,
shout, "See! This is larger, but no other way
different from a Junk Heap. Pick it up.
Cart it off. Bury it deep, Kiddies.
Rust is very, very bad for fresh vegetables.
Stop, naughty children! Oh stop playing in that goo."

IN POETS' DEFENCE

FOR VAN WYCK BROOKS

Rebel poets, who've given vicar aid
to murdered agitator and starved miner,
starve in your mind and murder in your thought
indignant will-to-help unfused with Revolution.
Nurture the calm of wrath. Though Labor fumble
a second Civil War, prevent a memory
like its first forged golden chain
to bind white peon and black serf apart.
    While labor power'd come too nearly free
in the open market of free trade for jobs,
choose from Concord conspirators their thoughts
which still remain Sedition; forget braggarts
after victory whose rage contrived defeat.

137

Not by old images of grief and joy,
nor mummied memory of the Civil War,
nor Mayflower Compact, nor by rebel oaths
which made the Thirteen States palladium
and shield and shibboleth, adjure ourselves.
  Now boom the double guns of Word and Deed
while liberal persons fall in love with ice men
and Wilson's ghost'll vampire Lenin's mummy.
Every memory of hope, every thought,
passions and nerves our stern philanthropy
with cheer, with eager patience for laborers' slow
smoldering of hate to crack down pedestals,
compact from bones and gold, of Quirinus and Mars.

SKULLS AS DRUMS

FOR MALCOLM COWLEY

When the *first* drumtaps sound and trumpets buzz
through doors and windows, then may no one stir.
May listeners keep their seats while orators
fear to speak to the point. In chalky schoolrooms
may schoolboys not look up; in bridal chambers
heart clocks'll keep "Tick-Tock" although the drums
beat to a different time; or the same time.

In the plowed field, or field of ripened grain,
may farmers look up,—and spit. However drums
pound or whirr, however shrill horns blow,
housewives'll make beds,—as usual.
Let men and women sleep with deafened ears.
  Only the timid fear not fear; only
a coward stops his tears. Father, remember;
remind the boy of 'bravery'! Mother,
entreat your heart! You who are fond of talking,
continue in conversation. You who are silent,
silently close your window; while heavy drums'll
rattle quicker to a wilder and wilder bugle.

138

When *more* drums beat and shriller bugles squeal;
armored hearses snarl around that tomb
where covered skeletons play with live corpses.
. . . Roll your great stone before the door.
(They will stifle breathing air
so foetal grey with funk.) Now, charge your wire
that'll bring a galvanic startle to their great
Jack-in-the-Box. Open the lid. Look in:
    Whoever stifles fear, he is the coward.
Gaze on the corpse, pre-mortified
—gas bloated—of Mars. And on the fearful
helm of Suicide, Inc., drum, drum, drum
drum louder to drum up more fear.
From fear *and* fear a sterner fear is born
whose name is Wrath,—a filament of light
in every man. O, snarling bugles!
Crack the great stone before the door.
Drill the fat corpses for a brave parade.
Send the brave skulls and bones under the yoke
with thump of muffled drum and trumpet blurr.

DEEDS OF PRINCES

FOR CUTHBERT DANIEL

Though few'll evade the mismated, sovereign pair
(primordial chaos and bassalian chance)
reject their measured nutriment of dread.
Clad cap-a-pie in preferable hunger,
make clear (before oblivion thaw your bond
in Civil War) that you'll guard sheaves of wheat
beside churned waters, and loaves of bread
within their ovens fragrant like cudding cows
while muted rumor whistle, as terrible
birds to startled foxes in the ravening
winter proclaim wolves' foreknown death,—

139

O patient children, born in crowded cold
from wombs of weariness. Command
all good in ken and nature. Dread not
union with common day. Break your
live sense through worm-spinning threaded
ancient cruelties, even on one another.

While boom the double guns of Word and Deed
any coward, though excommunicate from battle,
(with words under torture false as the deeds of princes)
tells *you* your decent loyalties in *their* wars
also in the slow fight that drops men with no blow.
Strike blind fists between your Quirinal eyes
(twin gods who feed on fear for Law and Order).
A wind of blasting light shall split your
mist to threshold dawn. Dawn's level tide
cool bathed, sterile of clinging memory
inundates your discovered, your own southward valley of class death.

WHISTLES AT MIDNIGHT

FOR JOHN PHILIP HALL

When factory whistles and the midnight chime
with echoing footsteps wash down streets like rain
toward opened millyard and workshop's unlocked gate;
Telephone Girls, pulling the plugs from their switchboards,
say, "The number does not answer." Policemen,
whistling along their beats, swing idle billies
and the firemen play at whist in their stations,
though echoed marching flood over echoing street
and fire whistles mock the stroke of twelve.

Some will go and ring each others' doorbells,
rousing the neighbors with "The Hour is here,"
to a night short as dancing, song, drinking;
and with East light, when the Army'll fill the squares

140

mustered against our second Civil War,
for the first bloodshed, offer their own bodies
shouting, "The Hour is here!" But quieter
ones, all herded together in barricaded
cellars, hush for whistled victory.

They shall come forth, denying triumph to triumph.
The streets'll fill again with duller footbeats
as, burying the dead, they write on tombstones;
"Soldiers and Workers! If whistle and whistle matched
as mutiny could rhyme with neighborhood
no Army would be found to fight the battle
in which you've given lives to half-matched thoughts."
  Moving in quiet upon massed machine guns,
uncovering rhyme-mates for half-rhymed thought,
while Word and Deed cog their cylindrical wheels,
sorrowers take on bravery.

HERDSMAN

FOR KENNETH PORTER

The cowboy's club hangs against the pear tree
    with a horn of a bull, above lowing cows.
Years ago the bull strayed away, and the cowboy
    went far abroad, to find him in the glade.
He went through all the glade until he'd see him
    amid cotton-wood snow, cooling his flank and dancing
    hoofs in the willow-cool river water.
The bull saw and charged. But the cowboy had swung his club
    and cracked off one horn; and horn and club together'll
    now hang on the pear tree, above the lowing herd.

REDEMPTION

FOR AUSTIN WARREN

Workers of Hand! Work your brain.
No more for every well-fed mind,
need thousands stupify in shrunk, sub-human bodies.
What do you want, who form our Army?
More bottled mayonnaise? D'y'want hamburger?
More beefsteak (like your boss)? More baseball bleachers?
Shorter (but duller) jobs; longer (but duller) loafing?
Such a weight makes the haunch of the footvault splay;
diaphragms cave in; translucently liquescent
no-hips slag to paunch. Ill-voweled
breaths from faces (unformed, but deformed away)
suffocate children's spring-rivuletting voices.

We, the Workers of Brain, work your hands.
Edictors of essential Doctrine,
we disagree, who may not disregard.
Does no breadgiving fill you with fresh hunger?
Trianon's lost dancing master found
himself among the Prairie Indians; and we are not dismayed
who'll fashion the pattern for the moral arts.
Take it. Or leave it.

Some men's salvation is other men's castration.
You, not we (if you don't like it) lump it.
You say you can run your own business?
(That sacred cause will exact unwilling martyrs.)
Seth wars to found the city which Cain wrecks.
Give your desires their necessities of form,
make yourselves into Fact whose continual revision
smiles in the mirror of each others' faces.
But leave us to our business (to be minding other people's)
and make sure not to board a wrong train for Beulah;—
(it may land you up in Englehood, New Jersey).

Seth's soldiers billeted on Cain
clear sidewalks of somnambulists.

Highbrows stammer approbation
compact from what others offer and we lack
extract from what we be and miss in others.
Even Lefts strutting like local cinema
cadets to follow Arrow Collar Eliot's
swivel scent of armchair sweat in armpits;
even the static stutter of Adamic (tone deaf)
who caught from swing-time of class struggle
cacophonous gangster rackets.
Even, and even, hick critic, Hicks, whose "*Be
revolutionary without being self-conscious*"
fully interpreted, fulfills the scripture:
"*Dear Daily Worker, Must we swear off lipstick?*"
Play cricket, hick critic! Hicks, kick off . . .

As music, sprinkling silence over sound
gives form to noise, so (once upon a time)
girl, spinning thread, boys hoisting sail
designed their song and dance from toil.
Soon likewise (and in no never-never land)
tediums' job will play, and boredoms' loaf
shall work; (soon, soon) work and play be recreate
and (shadow souls in worlds of shadow fires)
intellectual highbrow, lowbrow proletariat
forgot with battleship and mastodon.

Not like a debt-ridden suburban mortgagor
(living a life one step from everywhere;
who shudders at the rivers' too private lovers;
but shuns the unclassed, naked bathing beach)
welcomes the first flurry of popcorn snow-fall
to level alike his ill-kempt grass plot
with neighbor Jones' half square of manor lawn.
Not such democracy like even graves';
but commonwealth of planet, constellation
republican pluriverse, atomic star
deliver the ever-beleaguered Seth to powers
whose discipline is their emancipation.

Dominant sovereignties invisible
tangible brotherhood infrangible!
Smile in the mirrors of each other's faces.
And know all vital forces to look toward us
with the inscrutably inanimate.
Why? Have they not a better to look out for?
Post-proletarian, lithe Superman,—
ah! when they look toward him, we by contagious
imitation greet equal to equal.
(This never ceases from making,—it makes
rest; but itself never ceases.)

Vertical over flat existence
it builds in terrible maneuver
one rotundal narthex,—single-domed, unwalled,—
whose thirty-two-bayed colonnades
between the compass horns impale
refracted light out-dazing light's own source.
Its guardians survey its guardian void;
and, by refining deeds beyond the ever done
predict events' mere tell-tale shadow'll
point whence pieties veil their eyes
before the radiance of their servitors.

TRAIN RIDE

After rain, through afterglow, the unfolding fan
of railway landscape sidled on the pivot
of a larger arc into the green of evening;
I remembered that noon I saw a gradual bud
still white; though dead in its warm bloom;
always the enemy is the foe at home.
     And I wondered what surgery could recover
our lost, long stride of indolence and leisure
which is labor in reverse; what physic recall the smile
not of lips, but of eyes as of the sea bemused.

144

We, when we disperse from common sleep to several
tasks, we gather to despair; we, who assembled
once for hopes from common toil to dreams
or sickish and hurting or triumphal rapture;
always our enemy is our foe at home.

    We, deafened with far scattered city rattles
to the hubbub of forest birds (never having
"had time" to grieve or to hear through vivid sleep
the sea knock on its cracked and hollow stones)
so that the stars, almost, and birds comply,
and the garden-wet; the trees retire; We are
a scared patrol, fearing the guns behind;
always the enemy is the foe at home

    What wonder that we fear our own eyes' look
and fidget to be at home alone, and pitifully
put off age by some change in brushing the hair
and stumble to our ends like smothered runners at their tape;
    We follow our shreds of fame into an ambush.

    Then (as while the stars herd to the great trough
the blind, in the always-only-outward of their dismantled
archways, awake at the smell of warmed stone
or to the sound of reeds, lifting from the dim
into their segment of green dawn) *always
our enemy is our foe at home,* more
certainly than through spoken words or from grief-
twisted writing on paper, unblotted by tears
the thought came:
                There is no physic
for the world's ill, nor surgery; it must
(hot smell of tar on wet salt air)
burn in a fever forever, an incense pierced
with arrows, whose name is Love and another name
Rebellion (the twinge, the gulf, split seconds,
the very raindrop, render, and instancy
of Love).

    All Poetry to this not-to-be-looked-upon sun
of Passion is the moon's cupped light; all
Politics to this moon, a moon's reflected

cupped light, like the moon of Rome, after
the deep wells of Grecian light sank low;
always the enemy is the foe at home.
 But these three are friends whose arms twine
without words; as, in a still air,
the great grove leans to wind, past and to come.

AVE EVA

FOR ANTOINETTE KONIKOW

Wild strawberries, gooseberries, trampled;
sweet single roses torn; I hoofed to a ground
where a woman sat, weeping over a wounded bird.
"O silent woman, weeping without tears;
O weeping woman, silent on this ground
more withered than the barren; may I not help you heal
the suffering of this wounded bird?" I said.

"But let your hand first mend the axle of this wheel,
O scarlet-handed, azure-eyed," she answered.
"Let your eyes find the balance of these scales
fashioned from two of my sons' brain-pans."

"Woman with scale and wheel and wounded bird
more disconsolate than a child with broken toys;
first, I beseech you, uncripple this wounded bird
whose sufferings give to the mute universe
measure of its own pain." With no reply
the frightened woman, more frightened, for an answer
dropped her frightened eyes to the unanswering
eyes of a third skull between her feet. Then I commanded:

"Get up. There are more skulls hid than the three
skulls seen. Get going on your business!"

"You flaxen-faced and purple-lipped!" she cried,
"My business is to gather up my strength;
my purpose is to mend the axle and the hub;
and my intent, to find the balance of the scale."

146

"And . . . were the balance trued, were Adam's
dust, which was your dearest flesh and blood,
sifted over Abel's hunger-murdered eyes,—
should the scale tip; my apposite pan
I would then load with the bones of the warring hordes
of goodly Abel's brothers, Cain and Seth . . .
Leave your gray ground, Eve, go along with me."

"Satan," she said, "when my car moves, I move.
And the bird will fly. Its flight will heal its wing.
I, and my best sons, Cain and Seth, require
them who wish the bird healed mend my car.
The bird cannot be healed except by flight.
And when I move and my car mows the roses,
let dust and bone mold slowly close
Abel's insatiate, unanswering eyes,—
you azure-eyed, you flaxen-faced, purple-lipped and scarlet-handed!
The bird will fly. Its flight will heal its wing."

Then I departed as I came, tearing roses
and trampling the gooseberries and the strawberries.

THE CONCEPTION OF MAN

FOR MARY MARSHALL

When Elohim moulded red earth
images before Adonai,
Man was conceived:

Fountains of Time
rose to caves of Space;
Messengers cried: "Let Man be made!"

Watchers beyond (where spray
cannot reach cavern roofs)
cried, shaken with woe:
"Let not Man be born!"

Justice pleaded with Adonai, saying:
"Let Men be born, who, from abundance,
give alms to their sons."

Peace besought the Elohim:
"Let not Man be made
whose sons'll fight
amongst them for his alms."

Grace tempted the Elohim:
"Let Man be born
whose daughters, after battle
tend kindly them they wound."

Truth tought: "Put them an unhappy question,—
they could not answer whole.
O! Let not Men be made!"

"You speak," spoke Elohim, "We for you,
we reconcile contradiction. Earth
was not until our repentance
with the idea of Creation
cast shadow."

"Go, Truth, flow to springs," said the Adonai.
"Bear forth. Mingle among listening
Undines, so women, drinking, smell
the purple in the birth of thought."

"Depart, Grace. Hoe into solid caves," Elohim said,
"flaxen Gnomes engendered under corn;
that, as men eat, they taste death's hungry sleep."

"Go forth, Peace. Sail hence into the empty night.
Unveil stars," Adonai said,
"so while Sprites wink, men feel the azure of love's tears."

Elohim said, "Depart, Justice. Know that as you burn
you bring forth Lizard destruction
whose scarlet men shall bridle
building the undreamed!"

ARGUMENT

The Author's use of personal pronouns (*they*, for capitalists; *you*, for wage earners; *we*, for professionals) develops Lenin's grammatical example. His book, an essay in bringing good men forth, being intended for lasting entertainment, is didactic. Instruction which does not entertain does not teach; entertainment which teaches nothing is not entertaining.

If you will read the numbers through and after, if you please, each argument and poem (always reading as one reads the verses of the Bible, or for that matter, between the lines of a newspaper), what will emerge is rather more humanist than materialist, and much less a political treatise than a self-portrait of one who has found no way of turning, with Scientific Socialism, from a mechanical to an organic view of life than to draw from moral mythology as well as from revolutionary myth.

Morality confronts dialectic materialism no less urgently than it confronted the idealistic systems, for moral irresolution (with or without favorable circumstance) guarantees the triumph of gangster rule. But Scientific Socialism transforms moral science. Laissez-faire, trusting to control society through the aggregate of agreeable individuals, disintegrated the morals to which materialism is a lesser enemy than Idealism. In comparison to idealism, sacramentalism is materialist. Just as the Church through Scholasticism once squared faith with reason, and just as already Christian ethics have abandoned Divine Predestination for Economic Determinism, so religion (which is the social ethic of the imagination) must transform itself and dialectic materialism.

Because dialectic materialism is at least debatable, THE WORD IS DEED concerns itself with such a problem as: Which came first, the chicken or the egg? The distinction it makes between Destiny and Fate may be clarified by remarking how it is the fly's Destiny to live and die in the course of a day and how it may be the Fate of a fly to be driven against a screen by the course of a wind. Frederick Engels said in his *Anti-Duhring*: 'Act comes before talk. Talk of a God shut from the whole world is a gratuitous insult to religion. *In the beginning was the deed.* Act comes before argumentation.' Nevertheless, for human beginnings, the idea of an act originates the act. Ends form means. Dialectic materialism has its prototype in Jacob Böhme's mystic concept that a *quality* of creator and of creation is to *quail*. The inherent and spontaneous unfolding of motion in matter, its passionate

149

joy and tortured drive to act is the WORD of *Genesis* and John's *Gospel*—the Corypheus of deliberate moral performance which is a happy dance,—the Dance of Christ.

SOME PLANS ARE SIMPLE, a palimpsest upon a legend recorded from the non-Juridical *Tamid* states that we can not re-enter the Garden of Eden; whether by the Defeatism which is the price of the universal affection of a Jesus of Nazareth, or by the Imperialism which is the perversion in the strength of will of an Alexander of Macedon. The Author picked it out, together with numerous aphorisms, from Maurice Samuel's translation of Edmond Flegg's *Jewish Anthology*.

TWO TONGUES IN A TOWER (the iron tower of science, not the ivory tower of art) is concerned with the predicament of the white collar class, who see that the evils of the capitalist system (to which they oppose the goods of bourgeois culture) have become insufferable. Tabooed production frustrates their professions; but they doubt how they can advise the masses when wage workers shall become masters of abundance. They fear lest wage workers (who are so backward) may prove to have quite as little regard for culture as the capitalists. This fear and doubt may proceed from a fear of a future glut of intelligence; but at any rate, doubt holds white collar workers suspended as uncertain comrades in tentative and passive observation towards the proletariat. Although their class has supplied many articulate leaders; not their male but their female impulses are towards the Social Revolution.

LOBSTER COVE, an essay in pastoral, represents what occupied the end of a day at the Madame Goss House in Annisquam, on Cape Ann, while the Author was brushing up some chores for the Damons.

CAIN AND SETH were the oldest and the youngest recorded sons of Adam and Eve. Seth, the ancestor of Christ (born after Abel's death and buried by Enos with his father in the Cave of Treasures) is synonymous with the Heavenly Jerusalem, the City of God. The conception of human history as a war between Seth and Cain is St. Augustine's. The Kabalists felt it as the magnetism of Yesod upon Malkuth. The Earthly Jerusalem (or Rome or Babylon) is the City of Cain or Enoch, whose best citizens are its traitors.

LANTERNS OF TIME, provided by East and West with simple symbolic mechanism of Past and Future, applies for the working class against any totalitarian gangsters.

PECCATUM ORIGINALE deals, under their own mastering concept of original sin, with St. Augustine of Hippo and Dante Alighieri, two great political philosophers. Deceptive as Idealism is, Plato's idea of reality as Truth, which Fact struggles to approximate, is far from any necessary connection with passive quietism. Revolution, as every artist knows, is caused by its end and motivated by its objective. But in his *City of God*, Augustine, who was a Platonist, played Seth and Yesod false (like all who do not see that reforms such as those of the Gracchi are by-products of such revolts as that of Spartacus). Likewise did Dante in his *De Monarchia* although he was Aristotlean. Even Milton, in *Paradise Lost*, has not claimed for God-in-Christ the virtue which is falsely claimed for Lucifer, the Devil, Satan. This has been done by William Blake.

ANATHEMA. MARANATHA! which means "Let him be damned. The Lord will come!", deals with Malkuth as Stalinism, quotes the salutation with which in 1933 it greeted risen Hitlerism, and gives the materialist solution to spiritual problems of evil, which is developed later.

COLLECTIVE COLLECT is offered for all such as he whose "Letter to the Young Caesars of Wall Street," once exhorted pawnbrokers, peddlers and gamblers to rule the world, and who then proceeded to controvert the prophetic office of poets. He since bettered his poetic practice; but has suffered no deep political conversion. He attacks Wall Street, not the Capitalist System. Such persons serve the Furies, not the Muses who are of the Titanic race. Pegasus, the winged stallion (who since the Renaissance has been the steed of poets) was born of the dead Gorgon's blood. If we are to believe Francis Bacon, she is Tyranny.

Following in pastoral the propagandic example of cigarette advertisements, RESURGE FROM DECRESCENCE (balanced between dialogue and description) makes a woman, caught by intimate circumstances amid attractive settings, propound the questions to prepared answers. These answers continue the review of political thought which was commenced in "Peccatum Originale." Theological forms, which with St. Paul rose in opposition to Sovereignty, fell at the hands of Luther and Calvin more deeply than

151

at Augustine's or Dante's. Machiavelli's secular science, by exposing the laws of Power, is a means towards a liberation from authority.

BREAD-WORD GIVER, an invocation to the Author's immigrant ancestor, paraphrases the best known passage in the Fast Day Sermon which, in 1637, earned for him and for his sister-in-law, Ann Hutchinson, their exiles from Massachusetts Bay. Charles Francis Adams II fancied that this sermon was an original for MacBriar's exhortation in Walter Scott's *Old Morality*; but although it had trans-Atlantic readers, the seditious discourse was left in manuscript for 230 years. The immigrant Wheelwright's work for tolerance and emancipation ensures his lasting fame precisely because this work may never be completed.

FISHERMAN follows the *Greek Anthology* to remind the Reader how slightly work-habits differ outside big cities from those which prevailed outside the Piraeus, port of Athens.

CHELSEA EXCHANGE is a satiric comment upon Bohemian revolt which, despite the deaf ears on which the prophecies of Trojan Cassandra fell, attempts to set up culture in place of religion as a rival authority to politics.

SEVEN FROM FOUR makes an assumption that mastery over economic circumstance will earn all spiritual benefit despite our sins which (with Aquinus) are shadows of our virtues. Cultural and economic struggles are reciprocal and produce, through the imagination, sacramental blessings from material forces. Whatever the degree of truth in this assumption, we cannot get industrial democracy without at the same time establishing freedom, poetry, and truth; nor can science, art and liberty fully flower, fruit, and seed until the age of abundance come—the second reign of Saturn's scythe for grain and horn of seed. Even as a Host of mould, the Last Sacrament of Earth, can be given and taken in the absence of a priest; so this contrives the germination from Matter of all outward visible signs of inward spiritual Grace. Although "washed in the font of burning light" covers Water, Earth, Fire and Air; the correspondences are (as they must numerically be) asymmetric. Apostolical Orders are identified with the poets' function, which is to make memorial food from anger and from lust, even as it is the function of science to make fact out of desire.

TITANIC LITANY invokes Prometheus (whose name means Forethought) the best known and loved of the Titan race, chained to the rock, yet unhumbled. This shadow of the Saviour crucified is like him a type of all who would deliver Seth from Cain. The use of fire is a sacrament of liberation from material bondage through mastery over Matter. Here with Dietzgen, the original dialectical materialist, the Author contends for the union of the Tribes of David, the ancestor of Jesus, with the Tribes of Melchizedek, who (born without father or mother) originated the Order of Christ's priesthood.

In FOOTSTEPS the Author lays out the background amid which his self-portrait exists, lest the Reader weary of the portrait itself. Being written in voices, it is appropriate to mass recitation and makes little reference to established religion except by parody of the Lord's Prayer. Its thought is not Kabalistic and the action should be calisthenic. Whereas "Evening" in *Dusk to Dusk* deals through Christian mythology with objective and passive decay of society, FOOTSTEPS deals with the active, subjective forces of overturn. Its style is a continuation of the tone of "Alexander's Feast" by the Author's seventeenth century kinsman, John Dryden.

COM-U-NASTY PEACE is written in alternating voices. The first, that of the Newspaper, heightens the second which is that of the Seminar. Tammany Hall was founded in answer to Washington's hereditary Order of Cincinnatus. The doors of the temple of Janus close only when Rome is at peace with mankind.

YOU-U.S.-US (in the language throughout of the first voice of the preceding) takes satiric account of the chief difficulty in proletarian revolution, the subservience of the masses to war-hysteria and predicts how unfolding event will break this subservience.

The second stanza of IN POETS' DEFENCE (which departs from an oration by that flower of New England, the Author's mother's father's uncle by marriage, the Honorable Edward Everett) closes with reference to Quirinus and Mars, authoritarian Gods respectively of civil and of foreign war.

Quite as "Mossy Marbles" in *Rock and Shell* contradicts Oliver Wendell Holmes' "The Voiceless";—so SKULLS AS DRUMS contradicts "Beat, Beat Drums" in Whitman's *Drum-Taps*,—where naively he calls for a war enthusiasm so intense as to prevent any possibility of financial profit.

153

The Author contrarywise calls for indifference so profound as to germinate the civil war against war.

DEEDS OF PRINCES reiterates, in the language of the second voice of "Com-U-Nasty Peace" the central myth and chief intention of Scientific Socialism which is that only class-conscious proletarians, through their class death, can establish classless society.

WHISTLES AT MIDNIGHT because its movement is determined by the concept of General Strike, may be the most mythological of these poems. However as it takes account of the contribution of professional workers to the class struggle like "Skulls As Drums" and "In Poets' Defence" while being mythological, it may be factual and prophetic.

HERDSMAN, like "Huntsman" in *Rock and Shell*, (whose key words are: serpent-Capitalism; child-Culture; bullet-Revolution;) imposes allegory upon a bit from the *Greek Anthology*. Key words unlock the present poem on the political plane, which gives out the intention of the Bolshevik Revolution: cowboy—Workers; club and horn,—Hammer and Sickle; bull,—Production; herd,—Society.

REDEMPTION deals with grounding a culture under the Dictatorship of the Proletariat. Culture henceforth cannot rise under any other regime, and, once class restrictions are removed, the patents now withheld by technological taboo can command not only abundance but complete well being. Or shall future proletarian patronage of a public standard of sophisticated living (in distinction to the elementary demands of a private standard of living) be as half-hearted, almost, as present capitalist patronage? This fear may be the basis for some future anarchist revolt against socialism, or it may be a mere culture-philistine nightmare. At any rate, one can never be premature in arousing the masses to their cultural duties and to the joy of living.

TRAIN RIDE resumes the pastoral in palimpsest upon *Poems* by Stephen Phillips and uses as its refrain a slogan of the elder Liebknecht. The opening strophe refers to the kinetic dance of landscape as seen from any vehicle whence all objects in middle distance circle around centers which shift as eyes focus to the progress. The opening of the second stanza turns from a horizontal to a vertical plane by referring to the dance of stars at dawn, and to the applause of the vegetable world. The first stanza deals with the decay of bourgeois democracy; the second finds unceasing social change a reassurance.

In Ave Eva (suggested by the legend upon which "Some Plans Are Simple" is based) Yesod appears as the character of Mother Eve and Malkuth as the character of Satan, whose flesh is clothed in four colors which adorn this book. These colors of the Veil of the Temple,—which signify the four elements of Matter,—azure for Air; purple for Water; flaxen for Earth; and scarlet for Fire,—together with the gooseberries, strawberries, and roses from the 1629 *Journal* of Pastor Higgenson, and with the guns of Word and Deed, provide refrains to this whole book.

THE CONCEPTION OF MAN was written because the *Jewish Anthology* opened in the Author's hand to page 121. The inception of the poem was direct, complete and immediate; and continued what was indicated in these excerpts from the Haggadah non-Juridical tradition. In dissolving the duality of good and evil behind space and time, they present the implicit ground in mystical thought for materialist philosophy. Truth, Grace, Peace, and Justice, four Angels who have aspects of four-fold Godhead, are embodied in the Elementals: Undines (water) Gnomes (earth) Sprites (air) and Salamanders (fire).

The ARGUMENT has been concerned largely with matter. Let it close on meter. The Author hopes that the Reader finds this book more profitable in meter (as in matter) than Wordsworth's *Prelude* and *Excursion*. Most of these verses are iambic five beat, occasionally relieved by shortened or extended lines. As is natural to the English tongue, they count first stress and pause, then accent,—with only secondary count of syllables. Such prosody seems a private craft only to those persons who do not practice metrics aloud. The worst thing any meter can do is to deaden plot. The best thing that cadence can do is to liven plot.

English verse (due to the syntax of the language and to the influence of rhymed tags) is apt to run its color to the ends of lines. One is wise who by scrutinizing beginnings no less than ends (while bearing in mind that middles provide pause not only for breath, but also for thought) might contrive to address the will at the starts of his lines, the mind down their midst, and the senses at their closes. But, also, he might not.

Verse is an engineering of sound which, when it rises to poetry, engineers meaning. Verbal music and word pictures are ancillary to the mental music of governed association. All cadences are justified or not simply by their related sounds. The main point is not what noise poetry makes, but how it makes you think and act,—not what you make of it; but what it makes of you.

Annisquam,
Massachusetts,
July, 1939

DUSK TO DUSK
1914-1940

MASQUE WITH CLOWNS

FOR THE COMRADES

CHAMPEEN BICYCLE RIDERS quite
outstrip themselves to our fanfares.
They ride their Bikes backward tonight
with both feet on their handle-bars,
while the Calliope of a bright
CIRCUS PARADE hymns to Evening Stars
the investiture of Harold Loeb
with technocratic mace and globe.

Hearst in War! Hearst in Peace!
Young Hearst was first among country men;
but here we cease and there he goes.
So long, Hearst! So long as Long sang:
"Security makes every man a King"
Long was far-and-away the best
of RADIOS mightier than the Pen
all dressed up in Sunday clothes.

MILL FOR SALE
on Milk and Mill Streets at a Mill Town's end; one Mill lighted;
NO HELP WANTED
two Mission Breadlines move like sick snakes, round a legless Soldier
(who sells shoe shines) under a bent Lamp Post, with torn Election Signs:
VOTE SO.......and SO....IST LABOR?
Some Girls, reading: HELP NOT NEEDED turn aside
(squint, wince)
            make up their faces, and flaunt along the Breadlines, the
Breadlines turn their pockets inside-out; even a cheap Pansy finds no business on Milk and Mill, near Bogan's Old Distillery, pasted over with torn
Political Slogans:
REPEAL..EMPLOYMENT...WITH A NEW DEAL

The CLOWNS in swansdown sing a swansong.
Once we sang old words to the song they sing:
"In America no man is King;
and heavy the head that wears a crown."

159

But they sing new words to the song we sang
so fill up the glasses, drink them down;
Security makes a man a King
and a rotted tooth must bear a crown.

Therefore, while CLOWNS in swansdown sing,
let's stay, though Vespers call
us all, importunately, to an Irish shanty
where whiskey flows as free
as once through Tara's Hall, in Years of Plenty;
and where it only costs Two Bits (worth a Dime) to see
the Bonze of the bronze Shrine of the *Pansy* dictate sedately:
"Your Leda is your Leader, Christ, the King."

Priest, Long, and Hearst will be long dead first
before that means anything;
and as long will it be before we burst
forth in Plain Chant to a cheast
Broadcast; so,—so long! Long and Hearst; and, Priest
(so long—so far-and-away the first
of RADIOS dressed in Whitsunday Vest)
chant a different chant to the chant you sing.

Two By Gemini! elegant Girl Twin Six Day Motor Bicycle Cyclist ORATORS
(one a *Demirep*, one a *Publican*) wheeling in circles on armored mule *Elephant* and elephantine *Mule* impersonate the enmity between *Brown Derbys*
and *Slate Fedoras*; one flourishing *Gold Eagles*, one flashing *Silver Dollars*;
they clog-dance on neighboring Tables labeled:

EMANCIPATION PROCLARATION
DECLAMATION OF INDEPATION

From an unglazed Cellar Window of the abandoned Distillery, here at the
Town'send, flies a sex-starved CROW, his Beak blue Neon Tubes; long underwear sneaks over one black spat; from under his crepe-hung *Stove Pipe*,
he cries: "Economists who, like Jack Sprat, don't like fat really eat no less
than you or I"; he pecks the Original ORATORS in the Conventional Pants,
drinks a keg-full from the bunghole of 2% *Sales Tax* Beerkeg and reads
himself fast asleep on *A BEDTIME BIBLE*.

He is a Dry; he sleeps aloud,

snoring like a sty of pigs, and he dreams that Breadlines are unlicensed Nudist Leagues.

Mummy, is this Church?
McFadden, the Strong-Armed Man, blandishes Dumb-Bells.
Beware!
Monkeys leap-frog. A Tumbler stumbles.
His name's Sinclair.
And hear the Sorry-go-Round, and the Band cease to play.
Mummy, where's the Steeple?
How that bankrupt mock Music *Truck* rumbles!
Mummy, what's the Utopium of the People?
Sword-Swallowers, make way!
Mummy, is that the Minister climbing upstairs?
The *Elephants* now go round.
The *Donkeys* bray.
That is the Minister saying his prayers,
Mummy! Isn't he, Mummy?

First the *Social Light Party's* SEDAN CHAIRMAN with a gold-handled *Torch* (a *Social Light Party's* social party all in one)—with a *Square Paper Hat* above a Boiled Collar,—and how handsome (he's terrible, hysterical handsome) but as yet not yet as handsome as handsome Ramsay MacDonald was handsome, who once learned to spell every letter of

THE CHILD'S WAGE LABOR
and
EVERYBODY'S KAPITAL

He glues

UNEXPURGATED above A BEDTIME BIBLE.

His low *Torch* fumes illume the lamp-lit Breadlines who see him light a Candle (SO) and peruse

THE PROCREATION OF EMANCIPENDENCE

woefully; his handsome, shaking head extinguishes the Candle (So, So) with an enormous Pair of Shears, and Enormous Care, he divides-up one Banknote, one Footnote from

KAPITAL

and puffs the snips to the Bread-

lines, with a blown Kiss,—Unurned Excrement the Weary Willies miss.

Next a SHE SCARE-CROW (wingless chicken with Corkscrew Neck, brand-new Red Shirt, Infantile manners, diapers, and Disorders) comes trundling a stainless steel Perambulator of over-ripe Lemons; she tears asunder

THE DECLARATION OF INCAPACITATION
she folds Staleen's

THE LITTLE FOLK'S LENEEN
as a wrapper over

KAPITAL
shot-puts

A BEDTIME BIBLE

into the Lamp Post's Arc Light; and under a Shower of Gold (which all comes from Moscow) she pelts everyone with Lemons, and takes up a *Collection*; but she loses her Head (stuffed with chaff and straw) when she nets 17c in Valuta, crying: "I can't stand ready-made Union Suits, the Union Suits of Pollution! I ordered made-to-order Union Suits, Union Suits of the Revolution!" and screwing her Head (stuffed with straw and chaff) back on (wrong-way-round to suit her) she kicks each TWIN and the right and left shin of the SOCIAL LIGHT, who returns her *Co-Mewnal* compliments by slapping her wrist, turning into a LOUD SPEAKER and crying: "I am shocked beyond words! Love your neighbor!" while beating on a Tabor labeled: *REINHOLD NIEBUHR.*

Maskers stand guard with muskets.
Slack-Rope Acrobats, whose hair
is lacquered with chrismed scent
play Follow Our Leader, ogling
the silvery Jebbie, Coughlin
who minuets across the far
night sky's abysmed tent.
As he cries:
"Abra—Cadabra!
Anathema—Maranatha!
Hocus—Pocus! Ampersand!
By the Monstrance in my hand,
get those financial sharks,—
Friedrich Engels and Karl Marx!"
the Breadlines munch Soda Biscuits.

Two Rubber-Neck HE SCARE-CROW CHICKENS, in torn *Red Shirts*, faded to stromberry (one trundling a toy *Cannon*) scare the wingless SHE CHICK boneless by rattling *Sickles* along the Mills' Picket Fence; then the Right Chicken Wing and Mustard Sauce *Co-Mewnist Opposition* Club Plate Combination, with John Dos Passos' latest Tract:

FAIRY

TALES

FROM

RUSSIA

opposing the Permanent (tidy-wave) Left Chicken Wing and Radical Horse Radish Three-Decker Combination *Opposition Communist*, with Edmund Wilson's trot of Trotsky's

PRUSSIA!

THE NEXT?

AMERICA:

conk the Boneheads' heads with Tomes, heavy as bricks; and tapdance on Powder Kegs, with mighty-fine kicks.

What is that frightful noise? Why is no one
listening except Comrats, Brain Trust Dicks, and Hamilton Fish!
You don't mean that rumble from up Milk Street?
Is it only John Reed's Boys selling Gold Bricks to
MacLeish, the Agitator of Young Men about Town?
Do you know what that is, coming down Milk Street?
No!
Come and get a jag on the Anti-Marx Band Wagon,
christening with any drink you wish?
Do you think that is a Tractor rumbling down Milk Street?
Yes!
Lawrence Dennis Juleps flip your eyes upside down.
Rodman's Cleansing Fluid turns Red Shirts brown.
Don't you know that is an Amazon coming down Milk Street?
Yes!
Toast Young America, Nietzschean, but hearty.
Or
come and get a jag on the Marxist Band Wagon.
Isn't she a Beauty? the Tractor? the AMAZON TRACTOR.

Yes!
Cheer the inevitable Nth International. Cheer that
musty *All-American Workers' Party.*

When the TRACTOR, Giantess, stands where it says:
STOP, LOOK, & LISTEN
at the meeting of
Milk and Mill (gold-digging the *Elephantine Mule* in bestial flirtation) one,
who bears in one hand that Infernal Machine called a Ping-Pong Racquet
and Ba-Ba Black Sheep Balls in the other, gargles from a ticking Baby
Big Ben *Bomb* he carries in his watch pocket, makes as though to throw the
Baby Big Ben *Bomb*, but throws the Ba-Ba Balls instead which (being on
Elastic Bands) boomerang him Bang! on the back of his calked black
Pants chalked:
I. W. W.
He is a Noble SAVAGE. He swallows a Bottle of E. E. Cummings' *O! Me!*
O! My! Relax Tablets, and reads Percy Bysshe Shelley's unbound
PROMETHEUS UNBOUND
to BULLS, with
invisible Bellies under motorcycle Belts, and with whirling-twirling *Billies.*

Listen: the PARADE parts.
The Biggest-Navy-Yet President
knocks on the door.
A grinning mask on crooked stilts;
as his legs wilted, his grin wilts.
When he peeks in
his zebras dance with muffled thuds.
The wheels of Sicilian carts
sink in waves of paper buds.
He lifts the latch.
While sacred oxen chew their cuds
sanctimonious, as for Lent
the fatuous Strike-Breaker's hips
move, and his withered grinning lips
walk in:
hyenas howl. The fun starts.

"Hate to trouble you," roar the BULLS, cracking Steel Whips. Seven pointer-fingers (thumbs down) point the ANARCHIST, *chopped under chin*, taken for deportation. Untamed Lions tamed, the seven SILLIES; at attention, all in turn saluting; broadcast, all out of turn:

O DEMOCRATIC PEEPUL...
 IN SOVIET AMERICA...
  DRINK BEER WHICH IS NOT BEER.
REPUBLICANS BRING PROSPERITY...
 AND PERMANENT REVOLUTION.
REPEAL UNEMPLOYMENT...
 FOR THE WORKERS' AGE.

The wingless SCARE-CROW CHICKEN with a Cork-Screw Neck crooks her *Sickle* round her waist and, pounding the ground with her *Hammer* to the sound of rivet guns, raises a fire-balloon blister on her right big toe. The BROWN DERBY brays through the Maw of a DONKEY, the SLATE FEDORA trumpets through the trunk of an ELEPHANT, until the planks of each Platform crack beneath her Honky-Tonky (sound of Corks popping). The awakened CRAPE-HUNG STOVE-PIPE drowning in Twenty-four Billion Quarts of sixty year aged Champagne Cider caws: "Even Death has a Stick in it!" HE-CROW Quick COCK Rubber-Neck Right-Winged "Horse Radish" reaping deftly with the *Sickle* swaths his She-Comrade HEN SCARE-CROW clean in two! (There must be some Trick in it.) The SQUARE PAPER HAT to the sparks, glowing far, of his gilt *Torch* lights a KARL MARX CIGAR. My! What an Explosion! The SOCIAL LIGHT's OUT! Cacophonous Confusion!

GAMMADION! FYLFOT!

ANARCHIST AGITATOR and agitated BULLS, hand-cuffed tandem together, drawn in the Jitney Calliope CAR OF STATE, with Axles of *Fasces* and *Axes*, and elliptical *Swastika* Wheels; the Left-Winged Rubber-Neck COCK "Mustard" SCARE-CROW, handspringing, reels; and somersaults in Song:
 "Long Ago
 I told you So,—"

The Self-Starter has short circuited . . . . But! all on top of the double-faced Idol [Leda before and anti-Christ behind (which is on top of everything in the World)] flops, not the elastic *Papal Fig Leaf*, not the Enema of the People, but a paper *Rosey-Posey*. The Weary Willies mistake the *Little Flower* for a little flour, mistake Faith for Hope and Bread for Dope. The poor Weary Willies cheer . . . BLACKOUT,—

X

YEARS LONG

Two Mills for Sale

next Bogan's
Old Distillery; three Soldiers (who share one leg), white Floosies' sandals;
the Floosies read an old NO HELP NEEDED

ad, by the light of a Street Lamp,
whose Arc Light's gone mad; while a Pansy, turned Marine Recruiting
Sergeant, handles young Tramps' Salvation Army hymns, a new CIRCUS
PARADE begins (with the number of Gags doubled for double the number
of CAMPS):

Let's go! Vesper calls
all importunately
to a shanty
where the whiskey's free . . .

What's that knocking from the Mill Yard Door?
In spite of what the Barkers shout
and all the Bill Boards said,
I don't know.
What's that peeking from the Mill Yard Door?
There is no bread.
Why the Breadlines don't stop
I don't know.
What's that walking out of the Mill Yard Door?
It is a Giant DYNAMO!

Barbed thunderbolt, come, great QUIVER
of star-feathered *Arrows* tipped with corkscrew sparks,
for roaring BULLS deploy around the CAR.
We look not for super-men to free us now
as Perseus once freed Andromache
from the sea beast. Rather shall man-made beasts
free man from man by freeing class from class.

O DYNAMO! Your AMAZON
TRACTOR thongs CLOWN'S spines from pate to heel
with sinews torn from starved and murdered workers;
the cracked backs snap; the BULLS around the CAR
lower their horns; the circles of BULLS widen.

O thong the fallen *Torch* for Bow; *it* will not
snap. The BULLS around the CAR charge.

Three Arrows, in keen flight, zoom,
bite light, and fire the hackney SOUND TRUCK
with hacked-cross wheels; *Three Arrow-Torches* all but
blind the Mill Hands, streaming against streaming
shafts from the Mill's lit yard. Shoot, AMAZON!
The Leda-Jesus blackens without flame;
and now the legless Soldiers march on swords.

They fell the guardian BULLS and bathe the handcuffed
CLOWN in slain BULLS' blood; he who had clowned
in the Masque as SAVAGE, bathes the Whores and buries
all snapped spines; while the Farmers, pouring down
Milk Street, pile the Crossing high with good.
There, where they say "Stop Look & Listen,"
Breadlines stop, and look! there are no Breadlines.

Three Arrows wing, *Three Arrows* sing, *Three Arrows*
Three Arrows, *Three Arrows*, *Arrows*; Farmers and Millers
clad in star-spark-feathered shafts
with fore-arms flexed salute the GIANT ARCHERS.
But the MAN makes no salute, except to strike
his handcuffs on the monstrous MACHINES;
his handcuffs spring!
Unhinged, TRACTOR and DYNAMO
disclose ANOTHER WOMAN and ANOTHER MAN.

LIVE, EVIL VEIL

FOR DOROTHY DAY

The Church of Heaven's triumphal Car
by Justice and by Mercy veiled
(Car of wing'd, wheel'd Eyes
Wisdom's pulvery cornbin
winevat, bespattering, of Love)

169

steeled with mirroring moon and moon
whose spherical rims fall
desiring to climb, and rise
returning to their prime
(each eye-rimmed wheel, a wing'd eyeball)
clangs over empounded flame
with here a saw, and there a hoe
and shadows of smoke like flame.

Thin Wings wire the Crucified's umbra;
other Wings gyre,—His own;
the Pallium sails amid intactile fire;
the Shibboleth hovers over shadows
with here a sickle, and there a scythe
and here and there a hammer.

Shadows, returned to cover
three-fold, double-folded veils,
separately converge
into trine Countenance's radiances;
but starry Messengers behold:
their fires, to these fires, are
as yellow haze to gold,
their joyous innocence
to this lean anger, cold:—
with here a scythe, and there a hammer
and here a saw, and there a saw
and here and there a hoe.

The Eyes swoon while the Wings moan:
"Wake us from our repeating dream
within this clanging bell.
Search the unpaved cage
we pace confined. Cruel Eyes gleam
in sable moon and silver moon;
wake us from our repeating dream
of Hell."
With here a hoe, and there a hoe
and there and there a scythe.

Talons rage to claw the image
of the mirrored, iron Face's
clinging, clanging tongues.
Lion Jaws, to devour the other
(which is a mirrored brother)
call on crispate light to melt
prismatic wires, about them, of Mercy:
(with Justice, below, blackly reflected)
"Wake us from dreams repeated."
(They remain undefeated
recurring days; they will not die.)
"Wake us to fact; dreams lie;
wake us to Grace."
(These snakes, frozen on the waters,
were Wings.
These embers among dark cinders
are blind.)
With here a hammer, and there a sickle
and here a scythe, and there a saw
and here and there a hoe.

Loud, abundant strength of clang
—colorless, colorful, colorless—
(yet similar in righteousness)
shakes horny hearing
which once caused its song;
until, at length
the Wings revive. The Eyes awake.
The haze divides; the frozen Lake
of fire melts to spiral Space
where Justice (that doubles Satan's Face)
clung and clangs
as the hammer strikes, and the sickle swings;
and (as Watchers dreamt) it clings
to the Car's veiled Cross
in whose dead embrace
dead
Man hangs.

INSTRUCTION

By my infallibility in death
if you then act by what I thought and did;
all things I leave unacted or thought-hid
let swirl in chaff with un-skulled, jawless teeth;
now, therefore, swear by Jesus of Nazareth
(whose ministry to lovers ranks first, amid
unnumberable miracles) our bed
may stand warmed at your undemurring hearth.

Infallibly we answer as you bid
when we have loved. When—after we are wed—
there shall provide to argue, or to prove,—
nothing which now impoverishes breath;—
our wish rides anchored fast in the fast earth
by my infallibility of love.

FORESTRY

Your acres show your unfaithful spouse unkind
illkempt and victim to the bullies' creed;
and, like your tamarack, whom scrub oak impede,
is your trust in me with fears of him entwined.
War on your dead wood lest your dead wood breed
insects, blights, parasites of every kind;
cut rotted timber from your virgin mind
as we walk Indian file cleaning the wood.

If narrow shoes show poems and broad shoes prose,
my blundering admonitions, by your hints
liven my sense to mortify my pose,
and my wide tread can smooth your narrow prints.
No followers advance unless their leaders heed.
But you must follow. Direct me from behind.

IN THE BATHTUB, TO MNEMOSYNE

Away in this chambered secret, I'll draw sound
out of its cistern, pavement sealed, and drink
life water from rivuletted water life
of here excluded wind and sun. Intrude
your person, knock, or voice without a message
of great joy or doom,—I'll answer your sweet rattle
with unfond silence, or present at your fond touch
a hollow turtle shell, or vacant snake skin.

ESPRIT D'ESCALIER

That drop of sweat which is sliding down my mouth
tastes like a tear. Is my lip cut? was her cheek?
It was a tear, fool. Fool, you did not see
once through empty freight train conversation
her Jack and Jill tears fall down to defer
breaking that telegram her pulse was ticking
to her ears. They were, then, sweat and blood? Her tears
taste, in my mouth, of death and birth and salt.

I, when she ask me a question, or make reply
think only what I think; while she is thinking
our future, past, our present one dimension.
O! everything I'd say cuts with primal woe;
nor shall I ever tell the taste of my own sweat
from the tang of tears or blood, or taste of that spit.

DERVISH TO DUCHESS

FOR EUGENE REYNAL

Borgia to prove Zeno shallow
killed a thief with bow and arrow;
and, while shafts pierced his breast,
contended they remained at rest.

173

You, Duchess, follow Heraclitus;
your Christ is the perpetual foetus.
And courtiers whom you have kissed
proclaim Pythagoras impressionist.

But could you see more edifying sights,
our mountainous blue chrysolites;
from whom refractions, streaming high,
lend color to your filmy sky;
then you would feel two lovers lie
beside to share your single dream;
and hear birds' liquid laughing
pour over you, bathing quaffing
Time's circumambient stream.

If water lilies suck sublime
perfume from their natal slime,
what be the breath
of flowers grown in musk,
must wet with lees of wine?

Not Angels' atomic intelligences,
but humdrum man's,
put averages where the normal stands.
Who loses sight of Angels, sees
Wisdom comprised in moral formulas.
Ask him why he thinks so. If he reply
without disguise: "All is moral that is wise,"
he frees himself from atoms' tyrannies.
His mind clasps other minds with unbound hands,—
no more a neutral in the war of stars.

Your rubies, Lucrece, are but earth.
The sun fused their dull clods
with blood to burn
redder than lips of Gods.
Cæsar's pearls are only dew
drops fallen into oyster shells.
Enduring multitudinous hells

they to curling jewels grew.
What then must be the clean
hue of gems originally wine?
And what the shine
of pearl made pearl from pearly dew?

To compensate for Summer's green
snow gives your cypress brighter sheen;
but in border lands of time and space,
dropping sparkles in amber glow,
icicles and snow have place
with blossomed springs of indigo.

Go thither, philosophic Duchess, go.
Never hesitate lest you forever miss
the moth that bursts its purple chrysalis.

BOOK REVIEW

FOR WINFIELD SCOTT

Liberal lecturers, like Japanese toy-makers,
compress a whole culture to small compass.
When they wrap their lectures up as books,
I follow salesmen's directions,—
open the package, immerse the leaves
in my intelligence
as I would bloat folded paper flowers
on water in a dish.
They blossom before me,—each a marvel;
every one, to someone, a delight.

From such paper flowers, however,
one learns more Japanese than botany.

SONG

FOR SUSAN MELLON MILLET

Whales, leap Niagara.
              Sing:
        Checker Board
     however, otherwise.
Black and white kittens playing Dominoes
Clatter of malacca: muted Cornucopia.
. . . .

DUSK TO DUSK

FOR ALLEN TATE

Sunlight from under twilight
lifted memories of waking to tell:
"Noon shrivels our shadows."

Each, swung from each, dangles on string
(alone)
under the sun. Eye through eye
looks (not aslant) to ask:
"What shrunk us from each other;
even from me, my own black echo
my shadow, my slave?"

Glance not aslant, for all
shall soon; and soon shall
sunset twilight
tell of dark.

RUDE ARMCHAIR

FOR PHILIP HORTON

Once in a stanza abandoned by Hart Crane
waiting for you to open
your octagonal example of Romantic Gothic,
I thought of those who take repose in Depots;
I thought how negroes like new shoes,
watermelon and choo-choos,
and I nodded, "Good-evening" to an armchair
who had the back and shoulders of my own Father;
but who did not have manners enough to creak:
"Good-evening yourself!" by way of reply.

But at least, it did not, as you did,
produce that unemployed
Salvation Army Santa Claus
dressed up like Ezra Pound.

YOURS RECEIVED

There I cling to what is there.
What's falling around like ninepins? and what
lots of money it took to keep them up! You've got
one more security; you've done more
(inside) I mean. I mean you seem (outside)
just a peddler of toy windmills. Just
see, I put out my hand to see
really, are you there. What is there, really
to hold to, that stays to?
(at least, besides goodness and love that stay, at least
the same.) But would we, to each, stay the same?

YOURS ANSWERED

Yes. I put my hand out. Yes
I give to you in asking you to give.
Yet (unfocus) pet,
never wish anything to stay forever
put (refocus) Pet
nothing stays,—no one; and above all, love, not
love! But (in shine) waterfalls hold rainbows, love;
and ours, while sun is ours, the flow and
the bow. And we ask no change and you ask
for reason? For reason
let each take each for either,—let
the bow flow.

THE DARK BEFORE THE DAY

FOR HOWARD NEMEROV

They come at from behind.
They hinder from in front.
Never at any time have I seen them from all sides
curb my ears in telling
what my tongue would not say:
Fourfold between heart-beats
our counter-throbs sound not at all
because always the same.
Creep near where we nearer
quick and sharp
close the curving paths where the nether
short walls
end off short.
Learn all it means to learn
to hold upon spare want
imprisoned where you looked to sanctuary.
Let stillness penetrate the throat reclaimed to decision.
By the cliffs of preparation, you made yourself the stronger;
but by the shores of obedience will you remain as strong?
What once came down from behind
now creeps up from in front
saying heed our warning before other voices say
If you try the hinder paths
briefened by steepened slopes
the hugging hills will heighten as you climb.
From below from beyond from within
Look hard.
You have not looked where I am at either side,
Open your days as though they were crypts of flowers;
part your hours; find
I am found at either side.
Soon now it is the noon, the day's the year's and yours.
Look. Look hard. Become hard noon firm.

Cradle hours close; Light leaves you blind; Heat makes you cold.

A sky must ever bowl your platter world
While cactus open in the shine look through the guiltless glare.
Why do you drop your eyes?
What do you see?
Corroding grey above beyond within blue rotting noon
sky grey as dust
dust bright as sky,
I know what you are. You are my dust.
You drop from straight on top
to stay beside me on all sides:
moveless engraved in sloth and drained of hue:
Scorpions over shell-thin bones,
Serpents within bone-like shells,   *
lizards rooting among shards.
Lift your eyes,
The noon is azure (raise your eyes) assize when all your day is live.
Lift your eyes.
I dare not.
Someone keeps watching me. Is the whole sky one eye?
The horizon is all edged with eyes.
Or is but one eye at the zenith fastened upon me?
What is it looking for?
A sifting can be no finder than grey meshes of its sieve.

Hail Judas and again farewell.
Against the noon whose voice
fans azure dark without the green of dusk,
Hail Jesus and again farewell. Would you make me forsake you?
As I flee to go
ever I see advancing my future's shallow apse
and in its midst are carved why why why
the altar tomb of fruitless sacrifice.
My legs turn weak at the thought.
Wherever I am sent let it be
elsewhere I am not going. Why should I go
a doubter to carry deed to them who love only doubt's
rebuff to the caress of discipline? Why should I go?
Would you make me betray you, Judas?
Doubt which asks why, not how

come too close to entry enters the heart of zero.
But doubt denies my power less than your black prayer
promises constructed to remember life
so black as to eclipse desire
so black that angels' burning arrows drop
quenched in midnight amid afternoon.
Hail Judas and again farewell.

Listen hollow whisperings
stroke lips whom sundown darkness
pushes against hills
that open leanly tunnelled valleys of shallow water.
Listen glistening hailstones
listen the steaming rain spirals through seraphic orient
spatters the cliffs of sundered
hills and patters behind.
Thudding tremors tip the cliffs
while hilly rivers swell sentry eagles
lifted by the hissing lightning
vault to their embraces of all sides of the thunder.
Thunder fills its crowded hours
full with solid funnelled to prolonging.
It remains. But you wonder whither it wither
to clamber flatter ways and hold its winter snows.
It is upon me, I cannot bear it.
From before I feel it beside
come closer and calmer and clasp and ask:
What are you listening for?
Your hearing cannot spread.
Closed sound (though you hear not) bursting to smash horizon
                                                    bastions
throbs back autumnal tidal wave
remembrance and promise.
Shrink then to what you wish in space too wide without you.
Let us tell you where. Let us say for you look.
What do you seek for less for more for less
than feet and tongues inside remembrance?
We, the eyes and ears of the horizon
always the one unknown,

without you would not be.
Yet without us you were not here.
We stand at edges beyond the furthest hum.
But if you fasten upon us we destroy you.
Darkness smothers whiteness. Discover light mid darkness.
While fungus wither in the frost
though you hear the frost or hear not
till there sound the sound that sharpens light for sound,
dream what you remember
carved all round marble altars
lit by a tardy moon down looming
through sacrificial dark before the green dusk of dawn.
Early athletes training among ruins
shudderers who shutter each other against war
war-torn mothers giving their babies suck in tombs
and of these moon-carved marbles read the chipped inscription
decipher the chipped inscription
which when you saw before you did not heed.
In remembrances learn to die. From promises construct desire to live.
When you heard it all before
you did not listen.
You will wake later lustrated in lust
when the cherubic blue flows to seraphic red.
Now circles of freedom grasp you in their sphere
under the vault of obedience turn to kiss the wall.
Hush, This is lullaby.
Go forward we retreat. Retreat we advance.
Forward and backward learn in learning what you see how you see.
In any minute trap its brother minutes
who upon entering close the minutes about their entry
like the diminished divisions of shrinking gill net string.
You were stronger than we by the cliffs of preparation.
But by the shores of obedience we are as strong as you.
Desert morning opens
slow to watered
azure dusk (of love) before the assize of dawn.

EVENING

A MYSTERY IN THREE EPISODES

DIDYMUS:
—"Twin milestones mark a second mile.
With the far horse taking the traces' load
all the way our stallions danced sidewise."

DRIVER:
Minute by minute this hour passes
while the coming hour nears
when held by dim memory of creation
first all the creatures that first crept
and soon the fallen Angels cease from harm.

DIDYMUS:
—"Up this quiet country lane
nothing approaches.
Down the highway where the Faithful
sang this morning
nothing now in the still evening
follows after,
so why not trot our restive stallions
back to their warm stalls and stable?
Why drive them where they will not go?"

DRIVER:
The wagon halts! The horses veer
rearing not to tramp a Lad
who lies deaf to the iron laughter
of hooves upon the ground.

DIDYMUS,
dismounting:
—"He is all cold;
and purpled as though poisoned
he lies in his last attitude
as though asleep he covered up with a shield
his head against dreamt harm.

DRIVER:
"For this I drove forward,—
for us to see this gesture,
beloved of mother and father,

who in his childhood would come tiptoe
to see their child sleep well;—"

DIDYMUS: —"Gesture he will not change who lies
so still, so cold, so bare."

DRIVER: Whoever hurled these stones and glieves
hurled them too sternly.
Their bruises, like a martyrdom
show more excess than thieves' . . .

DIDYMUS,   —"Who killed this Lad?"
having remounted:

DRIVER: Out of its piss, behind
along the highroad, with a speed
that knocked its guts, a dread
Worm wriggled, brandishing its bold
and cloven tails but now fawning to your hand.

CHORAL WORM,   "Scorning longer to stay hid . . .
to DIDYMUS: We are torn to tell you all we did . . .
Reprove the doing and the Telling . . .
But we'll tell you of this killing . . ."

DIDYMUS: —"Yes . . . Yes? Go on! Speak;
speak; but speak one by one."

SELF-RIGHTEOUS   "When this morning (around
HEAD   Seven) we summoned the Black to worship
Heaven, he refused us, for no
Reason at all; to lie (at this most Sacred
Season) by the highway with this . . .
Woman . . ."

DIDYMUS,   —"You Monster of mechanic worthiness!
interrupting: Before he met your gaze, his seed defiled
neither himself, nor his Beloved."

184

WELL-PADDED HEAD:	"But I heard further . . . the Lad was given to a more perilous practice, even,— and among lemon-pickers stirred . . ."
DIDYMUS, *interrupting*:	—"Discord? I questioned what you did; not what you heard."
FLATTERER:	"Indeed unusual pleasure, these . . . Shall we call them . . . colloquies? as though with a twin god who weighs as Nothings all but accurate replies. Your answers, like bonfires, flame Rubbishes of all my days. Yet, pumping Pity, my severed heart Flies toward you as, toward sunset, Flies a crane."
CANDID ONE:	"From courtesy to women, we passed by. But when we passed again, we spied The negro lemon-picker all alone. And here he lies."
DRIVER:	You Evil, you! Although I found "Father" for the name of God; your evil name I cannot find.
DIDYMUS, *in secret*:	You are the Worm spawned by the horns who ripped the hedge round Eden's lawns whose slime rooted, radicule thorns around bread fruit when gardeners weed pull back, so dead so firm in the firm deep and shrinking as the bread fruits spread exude rot through milk-curded sap and the bread clusters turn stone with the trunks, and fall to earth and the trunks cannot burn.
DRIVER, *half aloud*:	'Yours was the claw in smiting Adam, tore North and East, smote South and West

185

(who once were natural virtues)
round whom you fell, with whom you coiled
till Wilderness, then Golgotha,
echoed with vinegar and gall
your tempted charity of stones made bread.
Your nod to your prey as "God and King"
is mockery of ministering:
"Fall from the Cross" (as from the Pinnacle)
"Fall down!" (worship the Proud).
You harden hearts to burden laborers
behind Peter's shoulders when to him
I say (as to your Father) "Get behind." '

DIDYMUS,
in secret:

Apostate to the apostated
Mouths who bite their tails!
(One within whom the floated
globe circles; and One all sea-encircled)
Never alone, you are harder to find
than these, lonely and proud.

DRIVER,
half aloud:

'But your evil name, I cannot find
though you be called Leviathan.
Evils work evils being falsely named;
I cannot name your evil.'

DIDYMUS,
aloud:

—"Most unabashed, now be abashed,—and stilled.
Listen:—the Lad you stoned
loosing your nameless Name
gives a stir through death, and speaks":

NEGRO,
to CHARIOTEERS:

"Who are these Charioteers
standing like tall still flames
as like as eyes are like
who gleamed and dawned
to my sunk cave; down, deep
where (faint) sunk light
adored the driver and the slave, adored
by deeps alone?"

186

DRIVER, *half aloud*:	My Twin, who as he stroked our snorting stallions, turned his yet unhooded head from side to side?
DIDYMUS, *in secret*:	My Slave white-cloaked, who raised and bowed his head within the hood's dark shade?
NEGRO:	"Who are you, Twin Gods, in pleated cloaks like fluted piers who hold each other by the hand . . .?"
DRIVER:	"Worm, hear the Lad you stoned. (Lad, we are Yes and No.) Worm, let us hear the story of your stoning . . ."
CRAFTY ONE:	"I ask you to hear; Hear me how I taught him Fear which follows act Which sickens, not acting. As the elusive eagles tend a nestling So would I have tended His goings and his comings. But he, grown calcitrant as mules Than goats more petulant Taunted: 'You are Legion, Worm, but I am one.'"
JUST ONE:	"Sure as our meek Faith condemns the arrogant So you would have heard (as you were judges, not the judged) Much of your own teaching in our Judgment rendered."
DRIVER, *to* WORM:	—"Tell of the heart these heartless served who cramp their hands to stone."
HYPOCRITE:	"Profane from the Word, We utter no unuttered Name. But need we? We are Christian."

187

DRIVER, *at first aloud*:	"Tell me no more!" Not stoned, poisoned! (Truth filters through half-lies.)
DIDYMUS, *in secret*:	When Lovers' eyes saw your Worm Eyes stare coiled round their Heads, Love, fouled, acting against such acts as one contemns in others sought for wisdom, ignoring her decorum your lids half closed.
DRIVER, *in secret*:	And when these headstrong lovers showed their love along the long highroad then all your eyelids closed.
DIDYMUS, *aloud*:	—"But then when the Woman left her Lad you woke to gaze on life asleep. You gazed,—and here he lies."

DRIVER,
in secret:
	Stern Sod, cleave beneath, tear
	     grand roots, firmly wound;
	Soil, hook the ankles, clasp the heels;
	     Mud, towards inevitable End
	drag twice twelve, twisted tortoise knees
	     into ice, twelve into brand;
	Linked, locking, jocund
	     Springs and, grounded Rivers, pound
	the Worm's lewd organs;
	     seething Gravels, grasp the navel;
	Rock, cold, cold Rock,
	     draw the heart to grind
	all the necks down.
	     Keep your mouth opened,
	Earth! crack your jaw. World!
	     swallow deep,—destroying Destruction.

DIDYMUS *to* DRIVER, *who* *slowly reveals* *himself the* *Crucified*:	—"Soon Governor; now Rebel from the Earth; our Deliverance; our Anger for the weak; Grape-picker of the live, Grave-Digger for the dead, at once my Master, and my Charioteer! I leave our car and my knees meet the heath.

Unclasp your hooded cloak; be pitiful; appear;
add Yes to No. First bow, then turn your head;
to signet the silent thought our Lad would speak
to vindicate himself to risen birth."

DRIVER, *aloud,*   "Get up off your knees.
having refolded   Brush the hypocrite dust from your knees.
his cloak: You lose strength on your knees."

NEGRO, *to*   "...Let me see again. Let me tell again
DRIVER: Let me. Tell me again
                      the Name of the Power of the Voice.
                      See; my lips make the Name.
                      Let my ears hear..."

DIDYMUS,   —"Be quiet, Lad.
to NEGRO: Asking for small things hurts the body;
                      and how ask for Destruction's End?"

                             II

DRIVER: Command!
                      Didymus, Didymus,
                      without command
                      Destruction will not end.
                      Now three, now seven, now four, now twelve
                      Tongues in Voices which sound wise
                      speak among them no accord
                      nor prudent hope towards their surmise;
                      and a Tongue who feels its feet are dead
                      demurs with hypocrite Head
                      in a Just Voice. Now Didymus, command:

DIDYMUS: —"Suck forth your poison from the Lad
                      you Worm, to your inevitable End!"

THE LAW   "But.....................Law's
to DIDYMUS: Destruction cannot be destroyed.

189

Your Lad's love stands condemned
    By the Law's restorer, Ezra,
Who would keep but a grape from a cluster,
    One ounce from a pound.
Are you not subject to the Law
    That you can come here to confound
Future subjects to the dread Last Day?
The Law ends on your side. Obey.
    Law's just Destruction cannot be destroyed."

JUSTICE *to* LAW: "Nor . . . . can Mercy's
Destruction be destroyed;
Mercy rules Justice's confounded fear.
Justice and Mercy at the last are nought
And (though the Last Things hold no scepter here)
He calls on you to nullify your Law
Who knows no Law in that which you call 'Law'
and dignify with attribute of Destiny.
There is Justice beneath Angels.
Is there none above Saints?"

MERCY
to JUSTICE:
    "Law, Justice, Mercy have to do with Time.
Time seems a little to Saints, to Dragons little;
little to us, Leviathan, who made men carcasses of Time.
Time is a memory and prophecy of heartbeats.
Life for the Lad is everything.
Rape him from poisoned Death to poisonous Life.
Show the whole Nature of our destroying fathers.
Destroying even Destruction."

DRIVER:
    Hear those labeled, unnamed Voices
while the poor Worm sink below its knees
and rage close like an oven these
many-headed slayers and accusers
who joined yet to one mother's
body, are born of hostile fathers.
All brothers contradict the others'
remembrance of their school days'
compromise, whispered percentages:

190

bold faced, loud-mouth and busy-bodied;
sophisticate, self-satisfied;
back-bite, back-hand;
worthy by rule-of-thumb, hum-drum;
damned muddle head;
clean mouthed, but none the less obscene;
hot loin,—cold blood;
hard heart, broad mind, dead level;
but-on-the-other-hand
just, prudent, clement, rugged, rude;
loyal, liberal, stupid;
conforming, sceptic, emptied;
mad grimaces shooting at your forehead
to uncurl their cloven tails and candid
smiles and find their doom confirmed:

PRUDENCE,
to MERCY:

"Yet . . . . .and . . . . yet
all Destruction should not be destroyed.
Our prudence once, in guise of Fate
Prompted Pilate and Caiaphas.
Now foolishly with Violence
As Cain killed Abel, we retard
A prudent growth towards Common Sense.
Therefore (as Folly had
Wrought Injustice to the Lad)
Render prudent Recompense:
Suck not, but drain, my Poison forth."

CLEMENCY:

"Let the Lad live, to see in froth
More Poison from him flow wide;
And ourselves be satisfied
To have our Principle abide.
Although not Justice, this would be
Law's substitute, called Clemency.
Destruction can never . . ."

DEAD-LEVEL
socking
PRUDENCE:

". . . never be destroyed.
Drain not your Poison from our Lad.
Interesting, suggestive, but unsound

191

Your line could hardly be pursued.
Breeder of the heedless, heed
All the elements involved."

CANT,
asphyxiating
CLEMENCY:

"Once others ask the thing you ask
Could we advance our common task?
You're but one seed of Father's seed
Whose high Horizons stretch so broad
Your mind could never have comprised
The All where all Poison, reconciled
Flows together at one speed.
Conduct all deeds that every deed
Seem universally decreed,—
Then can Destruction . . ."

SELF-RELIANCE
to DEAD-LEVEL:

". . . be at hand,
Infallible Leviathan (who call
'Inevitable' all that you fulfill)
You think you love, but you know you hate
Whatever you make wait.
Widow the Flesh
From wedded Soul (which you reduce
To a 'Resultant Force'). Enhance
Your 'Corporate Soul' (debasing all
Wills to mere words) words will proclaim
Your Doctrines of Ignorance
Chaos corporeal."

RUGGED
INDIVIDUAL:

"O, you are Legion, but I am one,
I differ, as each differs, from your Herd.
Had you but drained my Poison from the Lad
Your own Destruction might not be destroyed."

NEGRO:

". . . Now from a Voice of the Worm
I hear through the sleep of Death:
'You Legion, I am one.'
These words I said when the Worm
first crept as death creeps over slumber . . ."

DRIVER: The Peristalsis of the pronged Didymus,
           Necks flop like ript tripes on the prostrate Black;
           but over you these bitter seas, who roused
           their waves to cast you down, will soon
           lull, by themselves, their waves to rest.
           And when the Worm sinks past its Middle
           then or never shall Destruction . . .

DIDYMUS: —"end?
           How ever can it be mowed down
           like human fodder for Artalomes,
           the Plague, Death's son?
           Until the Last Dread Day
           how can Destruction end?
           Dismounted from command,
           my Head, with Worm Heads merged,
           I took no chance; now chance will lend
           no pincers to untangle dangled
           tangling of causes."

DRIVER: Do you live but for Destruction,
           dismounted from command?

DIDYMUS: —"I stand. One chance remains: I stand
           the one erected neck until
           (my inner argument self-killed)
           confident, I can remount the Wagon of Command."

DRIVER (at   "Why not remount now?"
first aloud): Doubting, disloyal,
           while the rock grind loyal
           Hearts, sceptic Tongues suck loyalty
           away; and from beneath the chairs of State
           exact their own from them to whom they lend.
           Self-doubting Didymus, while loyal
           gravel grasped the navel, Tongues of Loyalty
           within the Worm disloyal, frowned
           and bared the bottom of their State
           amid a bursting-bubble sound.
           "Remount the Wagon of Command!"

                        193

DIDYMUS (*at first aloud*):	—"I am a worm, no man." Pray, Worm, shall I suck poison from the Lad to our inevitable End?
LOYALTY *to* SELF-RELIANCE:	"Intransigent Minority, So rash with fact, Shadow Obscurity, Shade Unclarity Keep Faith at least with Fealty In prudent Act. Lest Doubt who turns about Turn your own doubt inside out, Subject in Piety Your own to others' Liberty That the Sovereignty of the Majority Remain intact. If we (the Plurality) Act as a Totality How can a Minority Get Poison from this Black? However can Destruction . . ."
SCEPTICS *to* DIDYMUS:	". . . be destroyed? Miracles, our Conscience tells Us, are impossible. Our Elixir must have been Poison to him to poison him. To suck Elixir now defiled Will bring the Law to naught until Destiny be called Miracle. We have no creed beside The Desert Gods' who fill the void Who with Destruction be destroyed."
SEMANTIC *to* SCEPTICS:	"That calling a thing *quid*, makes it *quid* They must believe, who ooze word fumes to addle every head. These misguiding lawmakers misguide

194

All faiths and rulers over every mind.
But our Oppressed are rebel. They have forged
redefinition of our every word.
Rebellion sees rebellion turned
Despotism as ordained
By Doom's predestined, undenied
Rule that commands as we command Mankind
Lest all Destruction . . ."

NIHILIST *to*
SEMANTIC:

". . . be destroyed!
We suck destruction from the Lad
When (behind words) the unworded word
Turns cogs whose chains, compact of miracle
(Catching in hub and rim)
Clog wheels which never yet stand still
Till cancerous Free will unwill
One Day all willed the day before.
Turn, therefore, Turncoats, turn elude
Wheel, turn and wheel again
And learn I bring to nothing Law and Laud,—
Of Destiny or Freedom make a word
That all within Destruction be destroyed."

DRIVER:

"The shoulders sink!
A Golden Grimace glows, all fear
lest, with command obeyed, all lose command."

PROLETARIAN
WORM *to* GOLDEN
GRIMACE:

"Weaklings, who suffer Victims' suffering,
Destruction must end so,—destroyed,
Self-perishing multiform diseased,
Lust to rule and to be ruled,
We perish utterly if we were freed.
Death is our Eatage and our Poison too,—
We Poison in the Wretched on the Earth.
Every named cause of every evil named
Shall be beyond your will when we're aroused
And the hour of fallen Watchers pass recall.
So, while you prosper through adversity,

Perform Mercy's impossible command
Destroying of Destruction is at hand."

DRIVER: At last, with double-tongued
                  despair, of neither hope nor fear,
                  the Worm now hails its brown withered and Satanic Star.

DIDYMUS: —"Now I remount the Wagon of Command."

All the HEADS   "Thou Porphyrogenian of Defeat
to their STAR: Whose teeth shall meet to lock thy final kiss
                  Invested with thy Power and Majesty
                  Loosed of the subjects to thy freezing heat
                  Shalt ride on thine engulfing, tideless sea
                  All unacclaimed in Apotheosis
                  Reflecting round thee, over thine abyss
                  Void, mirrored Triumph, like a Paraclete.
                  Sa-bar-than. Sa-bar-throbt. Bro-ma-nuch."

DIDYMUS *to*   —"Draw forth your poison from the Lad
LOYALTY: Put mouth to wound.
                  Draw forth. Take out . . ."

DRIVER (*aloud*): "Didymus:
                  Lips suck the wounds; the flesh turns white;
                  the whole Worm roars and swells to burst;
                  the gall pours forth. There where gall flowed
                  Earth cracked,—and down he goes!
                  Then there was a hubbub! and the Mob
                  runs away all over the place in a crowd
                  to tell the Miracle.
                  Open your eyes, Didymus. Didymus, look, the Lad
                  He springs up, and sees you stand,
                  and stands, and runs, and falls!"

YOUNG MAN *to*
DIDYMUS:

"... O! I destroyed Leviathan,
who exasperated me to what I did;
whom darkness canopies before
lest I learn what I do;
whom shame, conducting herself impudently
in idleness, follows after.
It was Legion, I am one ..."

DIDYMUS:

—"Be still;
the hour of adoration
for waters beyond the sky
descends round us. Be still;
the Seraphim's Trisagion
draws to melodious close.
Through the descending hour
we, even I and the Watchers,
grew still to the sound of the waves."

YOUNG MAN,
interrupting:

"...O! but I am the one who destroyed
the Worm who made me fear my deed
and my deed's end;
that I know now to promise Him
who makes things good to have
whose servants regret not what is done.
It was Legion, I am one ..."

DIDYMUS:

—"Be still.
I hear neither now.
I think that I see no Watchers
and in a world left vacant
hear none of the wonder they gave;
but when I saw, my Boy,
they still to me their sound
clapping each others' wings
to make a dancing temple for eyes glad."

DRIVER:

"O! Deaf to songs that live,

Didymus, smutty braziers
from pagan fruit-groves flare
flat flame. Cold winds bare
green-voiced lemon-pickers' mellow song—
But you abandon what you have
in what is gone."

YOUNG MAN *to*
DIDYMUS:

". . .O! I am the one who destroyed
the Worm, I am the one.
Take me with you, Stranger, Hand
me your mirror in whose glass
I see each read each mind.
I am without care . . .
Only, lo! I am blind."

DIDYMUS:

—"Nor will you see until you look
on your fellows with love in your eyes."

YOUNG MAN:

". . . O! Give me back my sight!
O, once of quiet, now of thunder,
return me what your mirror burned.
Once I liked to be seen, now I would see.
Give me, I promise . . ."

DIDYMUS:

—"No. Be still. Promise nothing.
In promises, you seek, like a woman
to gather strength out of weakness.
Take for yourself the memorable
splendor of desire graven on your brain.
Fears creep near them who outstrip shanks
in flight from gulf, whom I make pause;
but one come close who tarries
is nearer the destroying fear
never inevitable, always at hand."

DRIVER *to*
DIDYMUS:

and to the
YOUNG MAN:

"Didymus, have you yet lived
but to talk out Destruction's end?
Yes, Lad, ascend the Chariot of Command.
You did not fell the wriggling,
wiggling Worm; its power grew to the end.

198

Know eyes whence no act is miraculous
and hands wherein all things are miracle.
You will see. You will hear. You will speak
healing for governors; that the learned
shake convicts free; and convicts gather
captives again with captives
out of the gulf,—free."

DIDYMUS: —"Be still, you Lad, who turn
with questioning, from Twin to Twin.
Yes. If you say He gives you fire
you strike fire; fire is your fire.
Yes. If you say He told you the truth
you think truth. Truth is your feed;
be still; and look to Him; and not in vain."

DRIVER: "Yes. I would not let you turn.
I, the star of brightened
morning, open your blind
sight whom Didymus, dimmed
star of evening, blinded."

DIDYMUS: —"Yes. He was the first to taste desire,
He comes last.
No. I am the elder because born of old Eve;
He of the new.
Yes. Dark Jordan washed my mother.
His mother bathed in quiet light.
My father was of earth. His Father is of fire."

DRIVER: "Each answers to a magnet element."

DIDYMUS: —"Yet we are twins. My Lad
be still. You are to learn
twin twilights of the heart
and that two stars,—evening star
and star of morning,
are one star."

DRIVER: Now the near horse takes the traces' load.
                 Again mid-way between two hours
                 through fire flies and fragrant sound
                 Now, Didymus, be Charioteer.
                 Again to the laughter of hooves
                 drive toward the Beloved's
                 home into a day;
                 while across the gathering of the clouds
                 against the fears which ruled
                 the middle of the night
                 the Young Man holds the hands
                 beside him, all the way.

MORNING
A PARAPHRASE

FOR MARION CODE

THOMAS, *conse-*
crating the
Eucharist:

Behold God's body and God's blood!
The sacrifice is sent.
Another Cain, I shed my brother's blood.
Brother and God whom I (and God) abandoned
on a cold cliff to snake-beaked doubt a prey:
Eli, Eli, lama sabachthani?
My God, my God, have you forsaken me?
Serenest liturgy, intervene sacrilege
lest God and I hang strangled
on the Cross, the X beam of the quailing All.
Clasping the crux of its anaphoral
unendings, mid point of time and space,
we clasp their end,—O,—egg of nought.
Suffocated, with genitals erect
you caused the wide-staring heavens to wince
before your expectant, latter Fiat:
Let there be light no more.
But all you ever said was: Finished.
The sacrifice is sent.
Eli, Eli, lama sabachthani?
My God, my God, have you forsaken me?

ABIGAIL, TECK-
LA *and* KILAB
sing their hymn:

"Come Dove with seven circling doves
inebriate us seven-fold. Love's
cruxed flame and uncruxed flame match.
Brood over us and, brooding, watch
and ward the unborns' nest.
Hatch us into untimed rest.
When we crack the shell that harms us
of the egg of sin that forms us
snatch us midges who get dead
drunk with only six-fold loves.
We'll live on blood and living bread
doves to doves discovering covered doves."

THOMAS: Who taught you how to sing like prigs of Hell?

ABIGAIL: (Our lady, Teckla
                    who is crippled
                         whom we carry on her litter
                              to the Lord's Supper.)

THOMAS: Communal God, our communal meal
               wherein each guest think himself chief
               provides no one with common thanksgiving.
               Less thankful than in their breeding beds
               the famished number
               (even to number mankind in their number)
               seize upon medicine as nutriment
               and feed on cannibal taboo.
               There is manslaughter in the Eucharist
               you worshipers who importune your meal
               gathered to one anonymous belling cone
               the while twin candles fade against the single dawn.
               Unless your sufferings in sacrifice
               wed communal victory, this mere memorial
               is sterile holocaust and hecatomb.
               So O children, sing in common hymn
               for, though you lie speaking the words,
               truth speaks in you through them:

COMMUNION   The lips that taste here are made new;
HYMN: feet that walk here, walk in light;
               the tongues that sing here, speak the truth;
               eyes that look here, look on hope;
               the ears that listen, hear no clamor;
               and hands here stretched out
               hold the fruit of strength.

ABIGAIL: (The Bread falls from her fingers!)

TECKLA: ... The small loaf burns.

ABIGAIL: (She cannot bring hand to mouth.)

                              202

TECKLA: . . . Its stigma stings!

ABIGAIL: (She faints from hurt.)

THOMAS: —*Carry her close. Settle her litter.*

KILAB: "She is fair and lies in shame."

TECKLA: . . .I? I have always lived so clean
                   without a call to leave the world!
                   Which? Which the sin of which I am accused?

THOMAS: —Tell out what evil you thought good.

TECKLA, *while her* . . . I cannot. I cannot speak
MAID, ABIGAIL,   nor think whole facts . . .
interrupts:

                   (But she can tell how it happened.)

                   . . . Once . . . once I had no torment,
                   for I felt care for nothing,
                   but for Kilab, (my handmaid's boy
                   whom I would tease towards some fit bride)
                   to stand every other day beside my window . . .

                   (Every other day? Every day.)

                   . . . Every other day beneath my window
                   crooning, "Teckla!
                   Pleasing are conches
                   kept as clean as fragrant
                   fruit picked from dew."
                   for me to tease back, "Kilab . . ."

                   (Tease back? Croon back.)

                   Tease back, "Kilab,
                   flanks are pleasing
                   (pendant as pearls pricked in ear lobes)
                   who have flanks, though not having."

KILAB, *agreeing*:	"Yes, our virgin bodies, Teckla, are most pleasing . . ."
ABIGAIL:	(And she, to hear his fly song, hung tied to the window, like a spider.)
TECKLA:	. . . One day . . . one day as I came back from the bathing grove a queer man beside me, disturbing and disturbed, with a weak throat, made weaker query: "May you, love, and I, love, never be one in Love?" And big with pity, I replied, "My friend, I restrain lust. To you I'll give little." And I walked straight home . . .
ABIGAIL:	(And on the way she cried: "Abigail! my dear, did you hear? The young man how boldly he spoke!")
TECKLA, *interrupting*:	. . . I said "old man."
ABIGAIL:	(She said "young man." But I said, "What young man? That man was old.")
THOMAS:	—*Kilab be not shocked as her misjudgment were your fault.*
TECKLA, *while* ABIGAIL *interrupts*:	. . . Double-double points troubled slumber. With the dawn, I felt him slide inside my bed. I fled. But he came back . . .
ABIGAIL:	(I burned nard, ammonium, cassis before her door.)
TECKLA:	. . . I hung . . . rehung my mirror with withered leaves of bitter vines . . .

ABIGAIL:	(But with irrepressible modesty he'd sidle inside again.)
TECKLA:	. . . He'll never . . . never go . . . Will he?
ABIGAIL:	(Will she never get up from bed?)
THOMAS:	—Uncover Teckla while I wash her harbored sloth who cannot rest. Kilab, hand me salt and ewer. You, salt, from prime existence pure, mingle and melt with sulphured water, pressed through fountains of earth's matrix ash from fire's reservoirs. Consummate Dove weave your androgynous nest for sex of sexless trees, and rock, and stars. In minister and ministered nebular ovary of miracle made manifest through laws conceive by Teckla's maculate will a new born Teckla, gallant and fertile of womb, of maiden mind, and breast which fear of soil made sterile.
ABIGAIL:	(You Evil, let my Teckla go.)
THOMAS:	—*Poor Dread, you struggle to let loose.*
From the bed *the* EVIL *defies* THOMAS:	"Would you use force, who'll teach us its disuse? What have we with such as you, who have your own? Our bliss of death'll not come so. Until its present second, time had grown. What should we ever do with yours that you would have our own?"
ABIGAIL *to* EVIL:	(Spider, ill-favoured, misformed who wore down my well-favoured Lady. Frightful Evil, let my Teckla loose!)
THOMAS:	—Fretful Fear, struggle to let go.

205

The EVIL *mourns*
its departure:

"I'll leave you? I'll let go
of my delight?
On whom now shall I call to hear my tears?
Where'll I name thee a new name?
While you abide in calm asylum,
I'll seek your like to find her not;
faithful, I'll home, to find you as you are
(though grown a little older). Love,
we may forget the fluttered years . . .
But now, I go."

THOMAS *has*
KILAB *cleanse the*
intellectual Pas-
sages of EVIL:

—Cover the woman. Bring me
fresh dipped water.
Wash her eyes and eyebrows.
Smooth those tides of hair.
—Tell what you see, Teckla.

TECKLA:

. . . Did you . . .? Did you not
Watch my spectral hate depart?

THOMAS *cleanses*
the maiden fear of
bearing children:

—*I wish your lingering dreads dissolved.*
Go to sleep. Tell what you see.

TECKLA:

. . . a good . . . a gold man, leads to crags:
where bearded babies upon baby corpses
(swollen, like blacksmiths' bellows)
struggle. The plump flesh reddens.
The blood whitens. They'll turn
green beneath blue veils . . . Won't they?

THOMAS:

—*Clean Dread, dissolve!*

ABIGAIL:

(Cut a flower when it fade
or its seed to staunch a tree;
but to parch its bud, chary of fruit
were inverse husbandry.)

206

TECKLA, *still dreaming the selfish fear lest she lose her self in love*:	. . . But the good . . . the gold man brings me to a chasm cracked like a fissured corpse to sprout nine ribbons from nine caves where men and women, on dry mill wheels, hung turned from their tongues, or feet, or hair fumed with hemp fume and poppy fume grow sparkling lamps out of their glowing groins,— and none swing free.
KILAB:	"These bodies, pinned against this wheel clash (battling birds), for self-love must turn equal hate with equal lust; its limp corpse numb, though each part feel."
THOMAS:	—*Fair Dread, dissolve.* *We bathed her head in water,* *Kilab, her body in water salted.* *Bathe her burnt hand.*
KILAB, *to* THOMAS:	"As crippled saints are doubly victor but crippled sinners doubly crippled;— I forbear to touch her ailment. A cripple assaulted, she'll reprove me."
THOMAS *to* KILAB:	—Have little pity for cripples who fear healing. Crippled sinners are doubly crippled; but crippled healers, doubly victor;— Uncover her, and swirl the unsalted bowl in oil. She rises from her bolster. Wash her mount.
ABIGAIL:	(Look at her jump from her bed! She'll fall at his adoring feet. She grasps his hands to rise.)
THOMAS:	—Hug your embraces! Suffocate your necks! Now while I cense you; let the incense

intensify your senses' mingled lust.
My censer, as it flex and wilt
will kick fumes out like dust
off hooves of a nimble mare to scare
mongrel dogs of guilt.

TECKLA: . . . Love? . . .
(Even as you bathed my mount
you bathed my brows.)
Shall love for long
in company turn wise
that turned to fools' account?

KILAB: "As long as the long ocean blanch
against earth's wasting sand.
Love, when I bathed your brows
I washed my hand;
and as hands understand
love shall grow wise."

THOMAS: —Each lover thinking the beloved chief,
Handmaid and Minister to Mind and Body
witness while worshipper and server wed
one Sacrament trespass through Sacrifice
in thankful Thanksgiving.
O, Bed more holy than the Holy Board,
in fact of love, lonely dichotomy
(from complete pleasure to complete piety
in communal Baptism confraternal)
composes osmosis of love.
Now behold Man, and find no fault
Quicksilvery first pressings from twin seeds
bathes each body till its bones are bathed
and the too rigid bond articulate
     liberal, syllabic
moulds to cast shell counterpart
to shell, hand to hand, and foot to foot,
to manifest, how space holds more dimension
     than width, depth, length.

208

From male to female in-and-outer space
circles conjoined with junctured crosses flow
more furled than the hidden double river
     of the blood, whose trunk
and tributaries branch empurpling vines.
These springs' roots' clusters, and these
                         streams' abrasions
edged in asymmetry of heart to liver
     or like asymmetry of part
to part; or void to heart; in front to back,—
perpetual reminders, are persuaders
body to body how neither grows full alone.

ABIGAIL: (It is now time to go.)

TECKLA: ... Disparate once like snowflakes between stars
as thick storm clouds of ice encrust
mountainous evergreen until it creak
while all formed form dissolves into the forming,
must we replenish the diminished wells
within our nameless selves, abandoned, gone?

ABIGAIL, *hasting* (It is past time to go.)
the departure:

KILAB, *conducting* "Flowers, losing color to catch more light.
the departure: We grow by loss like a thaw's rivulet."

THOMAS, *in*   —As whisperings
secret blessing echo their Male and Female synonyms
their departure: inside shell-spiraled caps of spines
                 from ear to ear;
so the sexes holler to their antonyms
across the mountain (nothing) that divides
one from the one.
Links of these echo-forming signals
joining call to signal, echo-answered
double and melt
as cone to mirrored cone upon canals

whenever winds, arising to their seasons' chime,
ring fir seed odor over this old towpath of time.

DAGUERREOTYPE MONOLOGUE

Your Mother lies in her bridal sheet;
your Father in his soldier's cloak;
she, dead beneath the blinding sleet,
he, dying amid sulphurous smoke;
but you and I shall never part,
and each shall bear the other's care.

To hear heart answering to heart
until death take me, unaware,—
I smile always. In me you see
your Mother smiling, strong and mild.
Smile at me; and it shall be
as though my daughter smiled.

FAMILIAR

FOR JAMES LAUGHLIN IV

O, gilded Boston State House; O, gleaming Irish hair!
I saw Lady Bountiful taking a walk in clean sunlight.
A goodlooking girl, if only she hadn't lips for eyelids.
I thought I saw two persons, and I got all mixed up.
You see, it was this way . . . Lady Bountiful was modestly, even stylishly
dressed in two dimensions. But Lady Bountiful's shadow
had three dimensions, and crept behind like
pickpocket stenches of belches of Welch wenches.

STRANGER

FOR CONSTANCE ASCQUE

(While Boston blossoms into one brown rose)
how is it, Girlie, on your way

from Saroyan's whimsy play
Over the Hills and Far Away
to suffocate black incubator babies
that you carry a tall walking stick
embossed with the many-breasted Artemis;
but rubbed on its prepuce nether tip?
Did you lift it from my steady's mother?

OLD MARE
A. D. FOUR SEVENTY SIX

FOR THEODORE SPENCER

I have come back. I command my Palatine stable open.
Punctilious German grooms lumber forward to quiet
my varnished hooves, while a youth I have trained
to keep me amused with our daily game along the forums
of playing at trampling down Barbarian burghers
walks off stiffly to his rubdown, telling the others
how deftly I scattered the coin when the toll gate
keeper held out his till. My slaves' dull knives
scrape my belly. The slave who steals oats for his supper
soon now will whimper, "My wife has grown old;
but this Arabian mare!" That always gives the signal
for the other to make proud complaint how his Province
pooled its labored days to honor Rome in my honor;—
and that halfbreed stallion to whinny from the straw dark of the stall
the unconsolating mysteries of my inviolate vagina.

SAILORS AND A SOLDIER

FOR SAMUEL ELIOT MORISON

Salem, child of the sea, lightheartedness in hardship
called your men (like the voice of conscience) to the ocean.
Maritime voices commanded your most fierce child,
Frederick Townsend Ward, Ever-Victorious Commander.
It was Ward made the Manchu Army;—Ward, not "Chinese" Gordon.
Gordon was Ward's mimic,—ill-cast medallion
that steel event would stamp on Ward's metallic battalion.
But Khartoum dowered Gordon's destiny, and a destiny yet virgin
eluded Ward for all he'd rush (by sail, by horse,
by steam) in his career of speed to meet what flees.

Frederick Townsend Ward was born about 1830
from the best blood in Town. Aromas of amiable
Salem life around Ward's childhood were Cantonese.
Essex County houses, the food, (the housemaids),
linen, and the linen closet, smelled of smuggled Asia
although Essex Opium Trade was a most modest trade.
The Modest British contrived to keep first place
in poppy gum accounts of Salvationist Economy,
and in Essex' hive (through thriving days before your rise,
Salem, laid Gloucester low) the Universe seemed saved.

But Murray's harrowing of Hell and half-death's terror
turned into quack doctrine for Gloucester's Dogtown goodwives
who long at forest doors had dug for ginseng root
—quack doctoring for Canton. Salem, spouse of the sea,
plead that ginseng gold seemed more Christian than opium gold.
Those goodwives' years of death in slum decay were hells
of Asian fear while you by Asian rice fields, Salem,
played Crane among Storks.

Long before clippers towed our continent like a barge
(to the Lands of Prester John whither Columbus sailed)
Madagascar'd harboured through William and Mary's War
nests of Yankee pirates, who'd equip their ships at home.

So soon, had our granite land expelled these pioneers.
So soon, trine fortune rose from Niggers-Rum-M'lasses;
and punkas gratify a taste for drafts (which now
commands electric fans). In vain did sanded ink
close the routes our pirates harried for Revolution.
Sea-board merchants unsealed harbours wharves and drydocks
jammed with peace-glutted shipping, from ink-stained sandbars
shaken off rippled parchment to a parquet floor in Paris.

Why, any old codger whom Ward saw in boyhood
had sailed before the mast; doubled the Horn as a boy;
scattered contraband copies of Jefferson's *Declaration*
in the Spanish and Portugee-American ports of call;
bamboozled Manchu officials; made Polynesian love;
dined with Franciscan friars; and, landing in port one morning,
walked straight home as though nothing had happened.

Frederick Townsend Ward became a supercargo.
With a Phoenician job, he slept Macedonian dreams.
As a lad he'd monkeyed after the sea-dogs of his childhood.
Yankee boys, bonded to their elders' lack of capital
—with pinks so compassless as the Gael, Norse, Iberian
fisher ventures before settlers on Essex shore—
roved with astrolabe so crude (and with no charts)
deforesting Polynesian jungles of sandalwood;
and slaughtering the sea otter from all the Russian North.
In the far Spanish South, Aleutian seal-gangs spent lifetimes
killing and skinning a seal after a seal, all day.

Ward pandered to Mandarins for Bertram of the *Black Warrior*.
He dreamt his bunk a bivouac as he had dreamt his crib.
A privateer in the War of 1812, this Bertram
(debaucher of Red Injuns, Alaskans, Patagonians;
shifter of capital from ships to mills; mill capital
to railroads; railroad gold to copper) lived to see
the Stars and Stripes vanish, almost, from the Blue Water.
N'Bedford was draining Salem as N'Yawk sucked Boston.
Wage wedges (acute as blood feuds) crowded
marine insurance merchants' ageing whaler kinsmen

213

cheek by jowl with polyglot mob-butchers of the whale
who, every third year'd come home, in deeper and deeper
debt to failing Salem's rivals,—the drunken Quaker Whalers.

The Sea gave Salem meaning. The Sea was drying up.
Ward rose under Bertram, only to First Mate.
But on land there was always War. War, to be sure,
had not quite yet become our Heavy War Industry;
but War, as Machine War, had been revolutionized
since cabin boy, Colt, whittled a wooden model of
a nifty revolving pistol aboard an India Merchantman.
(Money era clocks, tick quick without slow tock.)
Colonel Samuel Colt "made a good thing" out of war.
Frederick Townsend Ward at last swapped smoke for tar.
To get as big as quick as Filibuster Bill Walker
might get in Nicaragua! Fight! Push things along.
Fight in the Crimea, now for Emperors. Fight
now for emperor-fighters. Ship for Mexico;
and fight in the Argentine, for Garibaldi-O!

Salem, greying haven (revolved in memory) return
to live days of '49. Ward's throbbing alembic
heart distilled its golden dust from ocean brine;
but chemically rejected nuggets of mirage gold.
(O Coronado) Then,—when his crew mutinying,
got a look of their Second Mate (a powder keg at one
hand, an emberous brand in the other) standing by
—short, plump, dark; with desert-sharpened eyes—
"I'll blow this ship to Hell!" O, soldierly sea-sound!—
(The sound of "Chinese" Gordon, commanding, "Nonethenth!
Tholdierth muthen't mutheny!" would have more sure sound.)

Salem, widowed of sea trade, your milk made you boy
(the might-have-been General Grant) who started as great as Grant
end great; greater than the Pandoran Perry
who'd opened closed Japan. Ward pinch-hit
nine wars and revolutions in nine years.
Just not great enough. Just scrimshaw technique.
Get great in conception,—concentric-not eccentric.

214

Emancipate Progress. Unslave Space from Time.
But a Yankee had to get rich. Try how that works.
Double-faced trade warfare (triple-faced)
anticipates afar life-captor's far capitulation.
One got rich in N'Yawk. Enter Pop's office on Broadway.
Let others work and fight; although the nursery memory
Caspar Crowninshield's Bucentaurian yacht
Cleopatra's Barge (built to rape Napoleon
from St. Helena) 'll make Manhattan business dull.
Salem scows (schooners dismantled) tote soft coal;
but Orient shores retain sweetish and certain tang.
Homesick boy (now home smells boyhood faint) what now
'll yet get one's self, grown strange, a stranger's home?
O be like Vanderbilt (great Vanderbilt
from orchid-ridden, lilac-hidden Staten Island)
to mount rapids of Isthmian torrents in a paddle-wheel ferry
with plugged safety valves. Hell! leave this funk behind.
Modern Titanic sons devour their parent past.
Ward locked up Pop's office. He fled the Civil War.

Salem, ailing by the sea, speak your turncoat's meaning
who had followed Red Shirts from LaPlatt' to Rio Grand;
but (when the tidal wave of liberation battered
his home's sea-mole) saw fright and fled the face of fear.
Just then Luigi Monti, Sicilian Risorgimentist
(mild, slender, blonde-wing-lipped, terrapin-eyed)
proffered Trade Unions and the Union, Garibaldi Red Shirts.
"Put down the upper class! Set up the lower class!
'Potawatomi's' fresh blood makes stale Forums flush.
Deposuit potentes de sede, et exaltavit humiles!
We fight a few Kings,—you, the millions of your Princelings.
Hail to the cotton-spinners' combat for cotton-pickers.
Make your milky Potomac turn red,—red like our tawny Tiber."

Lincoln saw it wise to decline Red-Shirt aid.
Luigi ate his exile heart in Winthrop, Massachusetts,—
and wrote a novel in criticism of our Consular Service.
But, still Risorgimentist, to escort a decent destiny
he'd blue-pencil Harvard Italian, emend Longfellow's Dante,

keep to Masonic truth; and he once told spirit-rappers:
"Crawl you back under the dark stone of Delphi
whose old Pythoness suckled young Yankee medium girls.
The white light of Republic blinds lizard eyes."
Today, Luigi Monti's tale at the Wayside Inn
with Enceladus, Mount Etna's gigantic captive, thunders:
"Put down the upper class! Set up the lower class!"
—Revolution's slogan from the Vulgate's Magnificat.—
"Deposuit potentes de sede, et exaltavit humiles!"

When Ward locked the office, he mounted his horse and rode
to Frisco Bay where, ten years ago, (before another War
—on Greezer Priests,—not this Nigger Parsons' War—)
five hundred hulls of mutiny-beached ships
served as brothels, hells or jails for crews, returned
Vigilante-manacled from silver-nuggeted Nevadas
—mirage-returned like empty-handed Coronado—
Napoleon! Bolivar!—O, Grey-eyed Garibaldi!
Juan Alvarez! Benito Juarez! Garibaldi-O.
Sail West to the East. Take sail again to lay
sea-learned knowledge of command and discipline
with bloody skill, acquired in battle on three continents
before China, the true China, rising from under the Manchu.

Help! In this most desperate, most destructive war of wars.
Twenty millions,—dead! Five hundred cities,—gone!
Feed the brilliant fire of Nanking's Coolie Emperor.
Help for Kings of the Rule of Peace, the Brothers who never retreat.
All the world's minds stir, till stir the mercantile.
Pan-ethos-archy of Han offered as good a "Cause"
(fit instrument) as ever given a soldier, spurred
with superb lust for glory. Their arms advanced. Rice fields
doubled. Silk trade tripled. Tea quadrupled.
Demand for opium fell. Our call of silver rose.
Whose working hell out of life would work a death of Hell
if not rebuilders (by rebellion) of the Church of Prester John?
Wild sons of our War-God soon invoked by Cousin Julia's
Battle Hymn of the Republic,—Ward never joined them;
he joined the Manchu side.

216

Speak, sickened Salem. Emptied, silent harbour,
do not tell the glory he might have made the cause he killed.
Speak out the interior flaw in your fate and Ward's.
Nor plead the simple limit set on nature, obscure
as the motives of God's only, Ward's doomed, stumble.
(Frozen crack in amber.) The fame in which he rose
will not rise with China. (Spider of frozen amber.)
Exonerate a hero, driven by immediate greed for gain;
but his fame'll not rise with China. At stated contract prices
(as one would bargain cargoes) he besieged and razed rebel city
after city whose blood-baptised Baptisers, stuck a-quivered,
hung, flayed, above their pillage squares day-long
and past all torture, lived, walking to be beheaded.
(Is this objectionable to our superior sense of pain?)
So asked an English doctor, answering for himself:
"Obtuse Turanians have coarse vascular nerves,—
and seem to suffer little." Ward mounted on river junks
howitzers Fremont had dragged across prairies,
and got thirty cities in five hundred days
(split by an envious British Admiral's term of imprisonment).
He beat the rebels down. The Manchu made him a Mandarin.
He beat down low the rebel brothers of his brain;
and the Mandarins gave him a wife (O, folded toes and lily
funneled shoes of Manchu China). The Manchu, delivered from terror
gave Ward a peacock feather, azure and green, like the Sea.

Salem; dying by azure, streaked, green, water;
return the mortal memory of a myth type, your Ward.
Like Joan of Arc, he'd bear no arms. He carried only
a rattan stick! Invulnerable youth! Bullets
spurted in the dust about him. One lodged in his spine.
He covered his dismay, put hand to belly, and said: "I have
been hit." His body stretched high in a Temple Yard.
(Not till our Boxer War, did we get his Manchu pay.)
A shrine rose at his bones. Twelve high lamps
hung as high as his relic lay. Ever Victorious Commander,
his rank as Confucian Saint is eminent as any
in the Grand Army of the Republic. His epitaph is lyric:
A youthful hero from beyond the sea

has sprinkled China with his azure blood.

Speak, Salem! Grandmother of the active who never
dared face repentance as your witch Judges dared;
tell, Salem, was Ward's spine shot by his Doppelgänger?
The boy, twenty years back,
acting Second Mate of the Clipper, *Hamilton*,
when under full sail, she plowed a Bengal Sea,
somersaulted overboard chasing a butterfly . . . .

DINNER CALL

FOR ADA RUSSELL

"Yes,—I am Miss Amy Lowell of Brookline . . .No,—I am not expected
. . . Yes,—I am paying Miss Dolly Brooks my call."
Her looks traveled the paneled wall,—up, down, across;
they could not rest on furniture adorning the wrong house.
But those framed autographs, Italian carriage prints, that
Indian deed smiled, "How d'e do?" from this best sitting room.

Her shell hands (assonanting her cut features) made her
obscene hulk the torse of an obsidian Kuan Yin.
Her brows stirred (—unsaid, clear-remembered, larger houses).
Her lips ribbed (—spent days, severed friendship).
For twenty years, a she and she had hung up their receivers,
—each for t'other to lift the telephone hello . . .

Now, while my Aunt and I were sitting round the house
waiting for the time to come for us to be sitting
and waiting for the time to drink our tea,
what brought her to Nantucket seven months after decent burial?
Digging up color for *Scrimshaw and Jade Fish*?
As she kept all the talk, and never paused once to say,
—I cannot tell.

"I'm traveling about at a great rate,—interviewing obituary
copymen all over the country.

And I'm sticking at my job to win the proper reviews, the appropriate
    notices for my last work: *Death is Posthumous.*
It's unfortunate that, for some time, most bright young things
    whom I would like, really, will really not like me.
But I must see no stuff-and-nonsense spread about, no tommy-rot;
    —my death must be taken exactly as I gave it."

When Anna carried in the urn, the lamp, slop-bowl, the pot, *et*
    cetera for tea, the Sacrament of tact; Aunt Dolly lit
    the alcohol.
Whereat, from that oracular orifice and steaming snout of repartee,
    the kettle's grape tendril of vapor gushed:
"Amy's got next the tripod of cookies,—great girl; she helps
    herself while helping others . . . (It's hot spit shut my eye.)
Let's let her let us help ourselves,—look how she takes up the
    entire settle . . ." (The lamp went out.)

"Well," (as she rose, her arms weighted down her armchair
    with dead wieght) "I must be off. No tea,—no belly-wash.
    No more, I kindly thank you, Dolly."
While Dolly rang the second maid's silver bell, there came a wind
    to shake the wild rose in the crystal globe. But I said:
    "I have an errand, too." And I went along.
"Yes, my blood pressure is better; and how is your death progressing;
    and do you remember asking when we met: 'How do you write,
    Miss Lowell, when you have nothing to say?'"
"That is unfair. You know I used the 'you' for 'one'; and as for your
    own tact,—
how about calling me, 'Mr. Brooks,' half the time; instead of just
    plain 'Jack'?"

Her eagerness to answer laughter made her stamp her little
    feet,—thud, thud, in the clamshell dust of the street.
As the lime rose, her neck turned grey, like stale ashes
    of cigars; but gushes of dead blood mounted her neck.
They flowed through her head; the cheeks turned red; the lips
    glowed like scars. But her eyes? Her eyes were frightened.

Our road forked; and she took one tine; and I took the other; and
    waste-lot Delta ragweed (fenced by granite posts and hickory

rails set diamond-wise) widened its wedge between.
But I turned for "Good-bye" to Amy Lowell, Biggest Traveling One-Man
 Show since Buffalo Bill caught the Midnight Flyer to contact
 Mark Twain:
"One would be inclined, at moments, to doubt the entire death!"
 I shouted.
Grinning from ear to ear, she shouted back: "Mr. Brooks, you are
 perfectly right;—one would be."

CROSS QUESTIONS

How do I know why you ask me, "How *are* you?
How *are* you? How are you? *How are*
you?" You do not care how I am. You
do not care who I am. You do not
really care what I think,—taking care not to, really.
"Do you, really?" you say, "Do you, really? Do
you think that you think that? Do
you doo? Doo you?"

How would I know if (in fear of fear) somehow
someone should ask you to bother to keep something
secret, you would not bother even to deny?
I am too busy finding who is not I.
Again? Do not start this all over again.
Please, I am still busy finding out them I please.

APOCRYPHAL APOCALYPSE

FOR WALDO FRANK

Wisemen to glossators unknown
when the Assisian or the Galilean
entered to the death which made his life
lustless in hope to find with keener sperm
have said:
"We liked him, but we found him hard to chat with.

His conversation bored us more than talk."
You gluttons for seedless speech and Vegex meat
who fondle terms to dull their definitions
and chew in vain each mouthful more and more
of day by day to find water taste sweet:
though sunk in boredom beyond excavations,
dose yourselves with bottled conversation's
pedantic antidote to boredom's poison.
Made of the Dictionary your Book of Truth
to hear the Apocalypse of Wheels with puckered lips:

Beware, beware like dogs with indoor faces
all fops and frumps who think it good, or better
for every man to follow his ideal:
anti William Carlos Williams Oscar Williamses
(less Apollonian than plumbers, laureate)
Waldos, un-Emersonian frank
Imbecile in paradisian beatitude
who ruminate on something . . . something
which men who lack a more definite term call Holy, Holy
wholly holy, hale, and wholly wholesome.
Combatting thought with thought's own element
Pied Pipers fop flute the Youth towards Baby's cave.
But above all Bores, the Hegelian Yes-Man Frump
beware who reconciles thought's hostile poles with smiles
(synthetic smiles) to prove his platitude
quite true: "Evil is the shadow side of Good."
God-The-Eternal-Bore-of Bores—subsists
in see-saw half-affirmation
(as A. E. and E. A.
Robinson have said at greater length
who each caught deaths of cold from Cosmic Chill)
but the Truth lives in contradictions of the flesh.
Transfigured bone can cast no shadow.
Something there is that does not love a Bore.

DEFENDER OF THE FAITH

FOR LEONARD BACON

While voices sift from the infrangile air:
"It's all okay, if you can get away
with it"; and: *"If it works, it's true"*;
broadcasting Nemesis of Faith Supernal
through the small membrane of Leviathan's ear,
Andean-towering amplifiers tell
planetariums to run backward to the day
before Pragmatism, becoming probable,
made salesman piffle a Third Testament.

The pin and hasp of Doubt once stapled Faith's
tackle to break Poor Richard's argument:
"Honesty is the best policy; but one who is honest
for this dishonest reason is dishonest."
Now merchant wits, credulous-infidel
(letting their will-to-knowledge slip and slump,
feeling their grasp upon our minds grow limp,
seeking to make our minds limp as their grasp)
run the planets' time-piece down, and say:
'Credo quia impossibile.'

And wearied of analytic manuals,
handcuffed in cool, Coleridgean clasp
they abuse Tertullian's abuse of Doubt,
and double-seal its lock with Newman's Jewish glue;
"What's easeful to believe, therefore is true."
O useful test of ease in truth, and easeful test of use,
O twisted Cardinal-Heretic's red tassel,
tickle our fonder feeling of belief;
tourniquet Doubt; and dry Faith to a fossil.

Religious Grammars have Positive and Superlative;
Primers of Science are pure Comparative.
Dialectic Unthought speaks no Grammar of Faith;
nor is doubt of Sciences' Doubt a Primer of Belief.

222

As, caught in Caps of Darkness, thieves lose Penitence,
so Christ's Church melts to Church Invisible:
thus only thus shall Hell's Gates not prevail
Never (if answered like the telephone)
is a Fact (transmitted once) an instrument
unfit for Individual Salvation.

Pressed beneath this, the Rock of Peter's parable,
swell seedlings of the herb infallible.
May vintagers who make their vineyards arable
banish their will from the Church Militant
corrupt in lung-fibre of commonsense
whose breathings voice, for social evidence,
eddies only, blown over stagnant bogs
and lamentations mixt with laud's
myrrhy perfume, oozing from the pine.

Twice born, transfigurated, triumphant
Faith, baptised in Doubt, rouse belief to repent.
Rouse us to stampede boring herds.
Rout their eschatologic analogues,—
Four Beasts who moo and purr and squawk and whine,—
about the Throne Intelligence.

1. *EAGLET*

FOR HENRY L. MENCKEN

While wrapt in wonder and their evening wraps
a swill select mouth through *Die Meistersinger*:
($ewing Machine? No Singer sang and Duncan danced
the Reaper through McCormack's Mary's Garden)
"Cow louse ally colossaler cow louse all
had Wagner, too, not been too harnessed to two wives,
as pictures are to reproductive function."

Men ken no wiser than Mencken's menckenizers
chicks of the Hofbrau Eaglet caged in costumer's

plush zippers with one green carnation
who (pontificating in the men's can) patters
like a bungled Bunthorne from home-baked
broadcast recordings of primordial mud:

"Fine Arts are less ideal than Poetry.
Poetry and Religion defeat God.
Poetry turning Music attains Beauty.
The trouble with the Arts is they lack movement.
One picture is a bar of Scriabin.
Music demands, of all the Arts, the most training.
The next harder is Modern Architecture.
Greek Architecture was a cinch, merely Design.
Pictures like womenkind should kindly make no comment.

"Palaeolithic painting's not as phono,—
as phorno,—I mean as photographic lenses.
Poet, try turning moo sick,—attain booty.
In a pitcher, a boo full stricture were a chore.
The next harder is moderne arch itch texture.
One picture makes one bar of Screech-have-been.
The trouble with all farts is they lack movement.
Moo sick demands of all the utmost straining.
No fart is more ideal than Poetry.
Poet, try and religion Gawd."

2. *BULL!*

FOR CARL VAN DOREN

Hear the Eschatologic Bull's bull calf
(brother in the veal to Mark Van Doren) moo:—
As Samos had its Aesop;—Indiana has
George Ade. As Scotland had its Robert Burns,
New Hampshire has its Robert Frost.' (If
this be criticism,—make the most of it.)

'Rarely since Sappho drowned has woman voiced

as keen delight in lovers as' (Guess who)
'Edna Millay. And F. P. A. like you
Gene Field, walks along the commonsense
Broadway,—like Horace' (Horace Who?)

But let the Bull bull on with: a. n. d.:
'Edith Wharton and Henry James; Melville
and Marion Crawford; Howells and Stephen Crane;
Walt Whitman and James Branch Cabell;
Vachel Lindsay and Stuart P. Sherman;
Henry L. Mencken, Edgar Allan Poe:—and—'

Wholesomest of Landscape Gardeners, Arthur Shirtlift,
Dorothy Norman you who feel about as you feel;
about as Georgia O'Keefe about Alfred Steiglitz,
you guess who, "Who, if not you?
Saint Vincent Millay!" Hip! Hip! Hooray
Associated Emancipated Women's Cubs
for hierarchic sex and girlies' uplift . . .!
Perfidious invidius insidius Ovidius Naso
Pallidula, rigida, nudula
Caius Catullus, Lucretius Carus
Whither, O, whither away?

3. *LION*

FOR WILLIAM LYON PHELPS

One pucker lipping Lion's whelp (in flesh
called William Lyon Phelps) purrs: 'After all,—
there is no Opera like Lohengrin!
My father, a Baptist preacher, a good man
is now with God,—and every day is Christmas.
Apart from questions of creative genius,—
there are no gooder men than our good writers.
Lyman Abbott and I, who never could read Dante,
still found Cathedrals beautifully friendly.
Hell is OK; Purgatory bores me; Heaven's dull.

There is no Opera like Lohengrin!
Miss Lulu Bett's outline is a Greek statue.
Augustus Thomas' *Witching Hour's* a masterpiece;
Housman's Second Volume is a masterpiece;
Anglo-Americans well know Oliphant's
masterpiece, *Bob, Son of Battle*, that masterpiece!
There is no Opera like Lohengrin!
In verse, these masterpieces are worth reading:
The Jar of Dreams by Lilla Cabot Perry;
Waves of Unrest by Bernice Lesbia Kenyon.'
(O Charlotte Endymion Porter! Percy Bysshe Shelley?
Helen Archibald Clark! O, women with three names!)
'Anna Hempstead Branch read all the Bible
through in a few days;—speaking of Milton,—
bad manners among critics are too common;
but gentlemen should not grow obsolete.
Often we fall asleep, not when we're bored,
but when we think we are most interesting.
There is no Opera like Lohengrin!
I sometimes think there are no persons who
can do more good than good librarians can.
American books grow easier to hold,—
dull paper and light weight is the Ideal.'

4. *MAN?*

FOR HOWARD BLAKE

Whosis? This Beast most terrible of all
because in form less bestial than is man!
How mannishly he shoveled Aristotle's
bladder gravel over Rousseau's grave.
Now with his calm voice bleached to a defeated bleat
emerged from moonlit groves to sunlit marts . . .
Do you think that Wheels will write on Irving Babbitt?
Then this is where Wheels fools you; he would make
necropolitan museumology
a funeral pall in cellophane:

226

An evil Boston woman loved the Virgin
with merely nearly mediaeval marvel.
When She grew old, She stuck together a junk shop
the texture of whose court (unfortunately)
inspired the taste of Alice Stone Blackwell
(I mean Alice Foote Macdougal) Restaurants.
Fed by her interior court's interior life
She lived off canned baked beans and cold corned beef.
She bore false witness at the Custom House.
Her "Guests" at restaurants paid their checks for dinner.
She threw nothing away. She was a mummy.
Given another ninety years, she'd have collected
Boston News Bureaus and broken shoe-strings.
As it was she gave good folks hysterics at the Opera
poking her magentad hair and ostrich plumed
monkey face at them between box curtains.
(Sandow received her and her friends stark naked).
She scrubbed down altar steps every Good Friday.
She had a Requiem every Christmas Eve
for the Charitable Eye and Ear Infirmary.
"It's not a Hospice; it's a hoax," She said.
"There's not a charitable eye or ear in Boston."
All this, because they christened her Isabella.

She took as lovers Boston's leading citizens.
Opera and Drama flourished in her Life Time.
Politics became brutal and dull.
All this, because her maiden name was Stuart.

Women, whose pretty faces had no bodies
women, with ugly faces without beauty
women, whose power depended on each other
said She was not a "lady" that no "lady"
with any moral sense, could leave cards on her.
But, She kicked up rubied heels, and thanked the Lord.

When young (because her things-in-law were Gardners)
She was invited to my Grandmother's Party.
Her footmen bore her light, white-satin litter

straight up the flying stair Bulfinch designed,
and set her down (thump-thump) in the Back Parlor.
Thus did She lie on lilies and roses
in a white-satin cuirass She could not stand in
with Parma violets at either hip bone
while *Men* crossed and uncrossed their legs all evening,
like bees who cluster round a honey cluster.
All this, because She said, she sprained her ankle.
The levee ended when her footmen entered
and my grandfather said: "Recumbent Lady,
I hope that when you come again you will be
perpendicular, not horizontal."

IMITATIO CHRISTI

FOR CHANLER CHAPMAN

High telescopes on highest towers show
that Saints and Doctors of the Church Triumphant
(or Buddhist Saints and Doctors, for that matter)
distraught from visionary docentry
see characteristics, lauded in their names
identical with traits, which they considered sins.

The elevation of the Carpet Slipper
to an ascetic Virtue is immune
to reasonable contamination. Love
of cynic copybooks of light housekeeping
seduced Charles Eliot Norton's wife's
bright little nephew, Henry Dwight Sedgwick
(pink victim of romantic culture addicts);
while he tidied up his tiny garden plot
platituded possibilities
of cultivating tastes for holiness
streamed through his head. No councils of perfection,
please,—periodic sympathy for far-off things.
Pro Vita Monastica. (Ra! Ra!)
Apologies for Dante to Old Maids.

There is no evil in cool summer sport
unless it lead one to the idea habit
that Saints of God are well-bred and well read
gentle folk exactly fit to suit exacting
Mrs. Jameson.
For once upon a time
and for all time
St. Francis of Assisi interdicted
philistine piety with paradox.
One irid pearl of poverty's louse-pearls
still rainbows fresh as that Seraphic Cross
who rained down prickles of his five-fold pricks
in feet and hands and heart:—intentions, deeds, desire;—
'Apostolic Paladins! Require you
no Book of Days; Theogeny; Book of Hours;—
no Hero and no Saint, basilicated.
Not one Disciple thumbed a Breviary.
No Titan read the *Works* of Hesiod.
We are the Paladins of Christ
but Roland and Oliver heard no *Song of Roland*,
and Christ has never imitated Christ.
You; you; and you are Christ Contemporary.'

ARGUMENT

Some correspondences between this book and *Rock and Shell* (*Poems 1923-1933*) give the Author an opportunity to correct certain of his critics. Poems labor nowadays under the dissemination of unfactual accuracies, for Poets are under an obligation to attempt the difficult which is not felt by the General Public whom most competent critics address. But the audience to poetry is granted by a host of simple folk who like to get facts straight. The difficulty others find in accepting poetic statement comes less from any of our poets' private practice of art for art's sake, than from public neglect of its enjoyment. The first duty of the literate is to read what has been written. It is only a secondary duty of writers to write what can be easily read. The "problem of modern poetry" is the problem of the market. No amount of talk about poetry can solve it, but as long as the problem remains unsolved, a good deal of talk is required from poets.

Let this be a fulcrum, lever, or whatever for those who use their ears, their eyes, and their brains to get through taste to fact; Poets write for people who know how to read aloud with wide-open eyes. You can kill two birds with one stone, if you do not spread nets in their sight. Poets aim at the head (they propagate, they agitate) but (since they find the root of understanding in the will) they address through associations the quiet wisdom of the sentiment in order to touch active reason. Poets exercise the will to understand,—by sights and sounds to teach.

Each of the twenty poems in *Rock and Shell* asks people to think of *other things*. If one holds to a course, tacking is necessary against a foul wind. (1) Before them who like pretty pictures, it brings up ugly thoughts. (2) It reminds the soulful of the Void. (3) It embarrasses those who want to be happy. (4) It chills those who love. (5) It asks Infidels to have Faith. (6) Christians to defy clergy. (7) Questioners should answer themselves. (8) It reminds them of silence who would have words. (9) For them who would be friends, it recalls enmities. (10) It asks the kindly to pity the strong. (11) It begs them who doubt their spirits not to wither their bodies. (12) Those rooted in the Past, it impels to feed the Future. (13) Those who love Nature to rule her. (14) It commends consideration of the out-of-date to the up-to-date and (15) revolution to reformers. (16) It pleads decadence to the respectable and decorum to creators; (17) prophetic conduct to evangelical titillators; and (18) action to men of feeling. (19) It warns them who look inward to look out. (20) While recommending politics to cultural

230

practitioners, it questions whether an individual solution of difficulty is to a mod-age no solution at all. The Author does not further an internal search for an absolute; but, contrarywise, the temporal battle against chaos for a cosmos which, unlike the absolute, can be apprehended.

The Author believes it a shame to deforest the earth by wasting paper (the air is free). Consequently he does not address the General Public (whose very existence is doubtful). He reaches the street corner only from the soap-box, and addresses poems to the literate. These (whether they be of his own class or of the proletariat) are entertained by dictionaries and read, not for rest, but for recreation. Not Hopkins, nor Rimbaud, Cocteau, Beddoes, nor Jonathan Edwards directly influence him. He is in no way descended from Bishop Phillips Brooks, who was celibate; the rumor that he ever followed T. S. Eliot is false. All *Rock and Shell* is religious; its successors are no less heretical; none demands great knowledge of Christian apologetic; the use all make of concepts is not personal, but traditional.

MASQUE WITH CLOWNS, which is in polyphonic prose like "North Atlantic Passage," the opening number in *Rock and Shell*, is a satire upon the electioneering campaigns of 1932 and 1934. The Author is dismayed to find little of it out of date. Its lyrics (transformed from discarded numbers) and its polyphonic passages choreographically give out the action of a revolutionary leg-show which was commenced in collaboration with a certain William Blake. The allegory (rising like Shelley's travesty of *Oedipus*, "Swellfoot the Tyrant," from burlesque to grotesque) is aimed beyond the conservative, not to say reactionary, goal of most satire.

LIVE, EVIL VEIL was started immediately after *Rock and Shell's* "The Inception of the Cross," whose penultimate stanza should read:

"The ellipse (not eclipse)
Of Hell . . ."

The ellipse as a distorted circle figures the dislocation of the Cosmos by impact of proud Satan's fall. That Evil's origin is theologically unaccountable gives a valid objection against benevolent Theism. But practical account must, nevertheless, be taken of evil result; and this gives valid objection against complacent Agnosticism. To dogmatic theology Evil is a mystery; Jesus' death has an eternal inception. Within this sublime nonsense LIVE, EVIL VEIL contends that Justice and Mercy (whose Heavens are founded upon Hells) cover up impenetrable enigmas to which neither

Reason nor Faith find answer, except tacitly, in what hangs behind the veil —vanquished—but yet unconquered.

INSTRUCTION and its companion are "correct" among this book's sonnets. FORESTRY refers to an anecdote of the Paris Commune when some one explained his presence in a workers' detachment by replying to a puzzled friend: "I have to follow these people. I am their leader."

IN THE BATHTUB and ESPRIT D'ESCALIER (which correspond to "Quick Curtain" and "Slow Curtain") essay to rhyme verses at their start and finish either by thought rhymes (such as *sound, drink*; or *life-water, water life*; or *now* and *then*) or by vocal rhymes (such as *to her ears, her two tears*; or *I, reply*; or *Oh, woe*).

DERVISH TO DUCHESS, composed in school-boy perusal of translation from the Turkish and Persian, doesn't mean too much.

SONG (approximating abstract painting) draws its first line from a bit of Benjamin Franklin's poker-face humor.
Prompted by Origen's "Commentary" upon the *Gospel According to St. John*, THE DARK BEFORE THE DAY of the mission of the doubting Apostle, Thomas, to India (a Continent of Doubt) is fit to follow *Rock and Shell's* "Forty Days," which latter study of priestly psychology puts in a good word for the lift which follows after doubt.

EVENING, following the best known chapter of the *Acts of Thomas*, gives political development to the universal allegory of a serpent poisoned by its own poison. Originally drafted together with *Rock and Shell's* "Twilight," it grew into a companion-piece to "Footsteps" in *Political Self-Portrait*. George Anthony Palmer suggested the strophes about breadfruit vines which come from a quotation in Darwin's *Voyage of the Beagle*; Grant Code suggested the ironic apostrophe to Satan; higher criticism suggested some other departures from the Nestorian original, but the parallel between St. Matthew's accounts of the Temptation of Jesus in the Wilderness and of the Mocking of Christ upon the Cross, has no authority but sense.

MORNING recovers from the disaster of the will which overwhelms "Twilight" in *Rock and Shell*. The meditations at the start and close, together with hymns, prayers, and songs (one of which comes from the Deacon's part in the Nestorian *Liturgy of Malabar or St. Thomas*) were drafted at Yaddo. "Abigail" means "hand-maid." "Kilab" turns up somewhere as a Biblical Abigail's son. The heroine's visions are condensed from the disciplinary *Manual of a Mystic*, which Woodward translated for the Pali Text Society. Teckla bears the name of a lady who is said to have formed a romantical attachment to Saint Paul. Not only in the apocryphal but also in the canonical Books of the Acts of the Apostles, St. Paul shares characteristics with the apocryphal St. Thomas.

DAGUERREOTYPE MONOLOGUE records some of the complications which overwhelmed us after the Civil War.

OLD MARE, supposing that Rome was run for her benefit, got no inkling that the year 410 A.D. should stand for the fall of the Empire, and this despite the destruction of the Sibylline Books by General Stilicho, who seems to have supposed that all conceivable catastrophes which they had prophesied were consummate.

The bird-house beat about the Author's ears while he was drafting SAILORS AND A SOLDIER (in review of *The Old China Trade* by Foster Rhea Dulles and *A Yankee Adventurer* by Holger Cahill). Like a surreptitious schoolboy he found himself writing prose. Time pressed. He botched his language, published the result as prose, and let poetry reassert claim to the material. John Murray, a British immigrant (1741-1815), introduced the Hell-denying doctrine of Universal Salvation to New England. William Walker (1824-1860), of Tennessee, made himself the ruler of Nicaragua where he attempted to restore chattel slavery. A descendant of Luigi Monti suggested in casual conversation the passage on that enricher of Yankee culture.

DINNER CALL's study of the involuntary envies which mar literary friendships departs little from a real dream. The wind-shaken rose refers to a ghost story by Mary Wilkins. The record of the Author's first remark to Amy Lowell follows fact more faithfully than that redaction in Damon's *Chronicle* on page 345, which should be on page 449.

DEFENDER OF THE FAITH corresponds with the "Gestures to the Dead," which close *Rock and Shell*. Its middle numbers are reworked in conformity to their mock meters from the Author's "Little Moments with Great Critics" (published by Walter S. Hankel). The last section distills a medicinal essence from a "Little Flower" of St. Francis.

ADDITIONAL POEMS

DR. RIMMER'S HAMILTON
ON COMMONWEALTH AVENUE
AND ARLINGTON STREET

Granite unsharded by the fires of revolt,
granite refined to the subtlety of a porcelain goddess of mercy—
common sense Hamilton!
Under the elms' sex-partite vaulting,
opposing the agitation of Washington on horseback
stands Hamilton,—

He has the stodgy dignity of a tobacco Indian
with his proud calf stuck out after the Bourbon manner;
but his shoulders, pressing forward with the elemental impulse
of a figurehead upon a Yankee clipper
(the *Invincible*, you know, that rounds the Horn in no time)
show us Hamilton, the genius of the Yankee
Ship of State.

The sculptor, Rimmer,
as he chipped in a crisp mastery the medallion on the pedestal,
thought, no doubt, of Thorvaldsen;
but his nostrils smarted with the native fragrance of ships' carving
with the nostalgic smells of Chipa hanging over the warm wharves of Salem
as he pounded the *esprit* with a mallet and a chisel
into the laboured, bare achievement of the staunch little spine
of Federalist Hamilton, the arrogant bastard under a prophetic mantle—
Hamilton,
troubled wisdom that speaks behind the mask of Washington,
Hamilton, voice of Sovereignty.

BOSTON IN SUMMER, WITH A CONFESSION

Neglected *Transcripts* on the steps of houses boarded up
and blinking behind diamonds, diamonds, hearts, and quatrefoils.
A fountain playing in the rain always shocks me
(so extravagant!) But then,

I was ever one to suck squeezed grape skins
and pour boiling water over used tea leaves.
Still,
should my summer pass without the glare
of orange paths, tropic palms,
and, in the sweaty night, swan-boats looped with lanterns,
I would flinch before our Siberian winter
and April dung storms.

NEW YORK IN SUMMER: INSOMNIA

Beneath trees whose leaves
munch the air like jaws
of alligators in Nicaraguan waters,
I sit,
sipping milk from a sherbet glass in the moonlight.
Trucks and elevated trains shatter the dawning.
I think how you have beaten your mistress,
my temples throb, I quiver,
though I would rather
be asleep.
Later in the year, when the light of the jaded moon is faded
the newspapers will lie crumpled in the fountains;
the dust will begin to whirl down the streets
in little typhoons;
the city will be arid, the window-sills grimy;
and the basins of the fountains half-filled with stagnant rain.
I have sipped all my milk,
the sherbet glass is empty but for moonlight,—
I must try to sleep.

CATHEDRAL

Within the ambulator of departed churchly taste,
amid the gloom the windows make of day,
the sensitive find sanctuary
from the city's jostled haste.

History is brought to life again,
Saint John's is being builded in a piecemeal way,
and we may see this church spread,
rising in towers from ledge to ledge,
as grew the ancients in the middle ages.

There is no religion here,
God knows.
Cast shadows, draftsmanlike, lend mystery,
there is kindly arcane twilight,
but no sacramental rose
glows before the Tabernacle.

On Sundays all this costly
archaeological architecture
fills the ladies with the thrills
of an illustrated lecture.
Each can pick her chapel where to skip & play,
while life is soothed with weeping,
the old tale true;
ranks of saints arise round Mary;
sin is sin; God dies upon the cross.

Around, the city stretches on all sides,
pulsating gridiron, mile after mile for miles,
unconsciously indifferent to the pride
of the echoing-empty pile on Morningside Heights,
save, now and then, for an indifferent smile
as they totter past on their buses through the wide summer night.

COQ D'OR

The fountain is frozen in the Plaza,
the little Venus atop
who has been squeezed out of a tube of toothpaste,
looks very much as though she had no clothes on.
    Silly attempt

                of some newspaper man to lend

conscious dignity to the city
with his own notoriety as the rate of interest.

"*Let us have peace,*" says Grant,
with the dreadnaughts smoking below him in the Hudson:
"*Let there be light,*" says God,
and skyscrapers rise all about.
"*War is Hell,*" says Sherman,
covered with old snow and sparrow-droppings.
Silly cursing,
for soon his war horse will be trampling
the borrowed wings and drapery of the gilded angel.

Soon the city will be swathed again in bunting
flopping with flags which look like pieces of awning
with their corners torn out.
This is what the newspapers whisper
as they rustle on the benches;
They want war.
Soon they will be shrieking it in the voices of a million urchins.
What they say, goes.

"*Ha-ha-ha! Hee! Hee!*"
cries the Coq d'Or a-top the Hecksher building.
Soon this card city of the Vanderbilts,
will be tumbling about us.

MIDWINTER WALK

What heather is parading the Fenway in a mist
with leather yellow that is fading, mingling with amethyst?
Tips of branches! Trees in winter! As I stumble, plunder, crush
through the nimble leaves I wonder
why it is ever said the trees are dead—
I can never take it in. The trees are wading naked
in translucent waves of underbrush.

Most beautiful, most Tuscan, most useless
Public Building in America:
I have walked the breadth of your broad plinth in winter rain;
with S. S. Pierce's spiced steam floating from Germanic roofs behind you;
with long shafts splintering on your Yankee granite steps
from your Parisian-twisted iron dandelion lanterns;
and I have longed to be Duke of Boston
(Wop Boss of Paddy Bosses) if only I might inhabit
your stateliness to hold court in your chambers.
Mauve and inquisitorial, that great horned toad
of a Trinity Church inquires after me:
but I moving-picture myself installing the hysterical Bacchante
(banished by prurience to the Metropolitan's House of Correction)
to liven with a sunlit sparkling your dun courtyard.
I would station a Negro row of First Corps Cadet white tunics
either side the melon marble stairway mounting to my dais.
I would set up an altar for your robe-enveloped triple God's
three-fold crucifixion, that, like an engine of warfare,
subdues all suppliants. At the Feast of the Resurrection's
orgies of Vodvil clap-trap, your garret galleries would echo
with tinkle and scrape of chamber music and ringing
ripple of tittles of women . . . .
                    But, upon reconsideration
I ponder the composition of the constituencies of my assassinators
—*kleinstaedtisch* fellow burghers of my Boston Brahmins—
who, while deploring the tactics of Cardinal Big Bull's "Charities,"
still concede: "He keeps the lower classes in good order."
They, who safeguard their wealth against the Enlightenment's dictatorship,
would do to me what was done to Wesley Everest, gentleman Wobbly,
castrated, buried in chains, from a trestle bridge in Oregon.
They who were hardly persuaded not to do the little boys
(who are not little girls) and who support
Sigillum Urbis Bostoniensis a very great injury:
"Knock the balls off. Tut, tut!"
shaking their heads as they passed beneath an innocent nudity
mirrored any summer afternoon on the agitated surface of the Frog Pond.

TALK WITH ROBERT HILLYER

"Across the basin slap through all directions
Billows of basalt in gay multitudes
And checkered shadows cross-cut tall reflections
Flecking the gulls who toss about, like gourds."

"The bridge, a bow, rejoices and, resounding
With all its lights and turrets, scrapes the sky;
Whips and caresses, cries too clear for sounding—"

"Why do we labor with these metaphors?
Monet, Whistler, and both of us are bores—
In your hair, also, is a Hokusai!"

MORE STRAITLY THAN A VOW

They go divided ways since those days were
when all his surety he gave to her
and sent her through the maze
straight down direct pathways.

Between them lies the world
like a cold sword.

And her refusal now
more straitly than a vow
will hinder them from love again.

PLATE GLASS MEMBRANE

Behind plate glass, the Dictionary.
(Book of Books). Below the Book, the Caption:
Every sealed book can be opened;
Else it would not have been sealed.

I saw the plate glass window;
I saw the specific weight;
I saw a sound like bells;
I saw the window break.

My nostrils filled with fur of glass.
Glass dissolved in seeing.
I saw all there is to see.
There was nothing to see but seeing.

I smelt the broken world of splintering words;
Knowledge, and nothing to know;
Light, and nothing to see.
Void would spell all meaning's undertow:

No sealed book would be sealed
Could all seals be broken.

A SMALL PRIG IN A BIG SQUARE

Dizzy from hot, long blasts of pulpit breath;
numb too, from having sat too still too long for a small boy
through Sunday meeting in the Eliot Meeting House
(so labeled for an Apostle to the Praying Indians
to americanize those interesting immigrants
who even then, flooding up level conduit valleys,
had quarried away the drumlin pudding stone
of once proud Roxbury) well, still dizzy
I remember, I remember, how I said to Pa
as we walked home in lustered Sunday shoes to Sunday dinner
how it was my belief how, some day, there would be:
no thundering El, nor rumbling Sub; no chu-chus; up-chuck alleys;
nor burping minarets like factory chimneys;
some day, no mucker Paddies; and all the world, some day
a Nice Boys' Outing Class in Franklin Park.

Partly because I got this off, partly because I thought
that it would sound (something) like something he'd said he thought;

I turned numb-er and dizzier when I heard Pa say:
You do, do you? Well then, you are mistaken.
The world cannot slide backwards, like a toy electric train.
Something's going to break; but clergymen won't break it.
There'll be more common people (more religion, maybe)
more distribution, more production, and more recreation;
but there will be damned less Idealism.
Get down to earth. I'm glad of any change.
But I shan't live to see a change that matters.
Dizzier, numb-er, I wondered, when *would* Pa die,—
he smiling at me like that; and to you, my laughing
brother, March. You, who were not an intellectual.

STATE OF MAINE

"How de do, Cap'ain Jones. How's things?"
Not so good. "Sorry to hear it. What's the matter?"

Nothin's no good no how; and there aint no God.
That's what's the matter . . . .

No price for lobster, cause of the Herrin-Chokers.
An the herrin don't run. Corn's got the weavel.
Wife's ailin. Ptatoes all rotted.
Daughter's knocked up.
Cow's dead. That's what's the matter.

D'AUTRE TEMPS

My mother—Bessie—tells the story;
after their precise lipping of coffee and liquor
ladies and gentlemen in Old Boston
as the gas jets all blinked low
(glancing up, opening their eyes wide
each at the middle of his-or-hers vis-à-vis visage)
simultaneously would concur

that there was yet time to descend
to drive promptly to the play
for in the Boston Museum the great chandelier
had jumped into glory;

or, was it in the Grand Opera House
or Papanti's dance hall with the spring floor
is it a tale of Old New York
or, perhaps, Philadelphia? Or yet Charlestown—
In any event,
this ill-remembered bit of misinformation
speaks of a time to me, of an America
not yet quite insensitive to all scale in life—

  2 CONTESTANTS CROAK FROM BLOODGUSH
      AFTER 6 DAY BICYCLE RACE IN
        MADISON SQUARE GARDEN

which is (it is to be observed) directly
across from the S. P. C. A.

A POEM BY DAVID McCORD

A poem by David McCord from the Boston Transcript
deals with Orson Welles' radio War between the Worlds,
during which the Communists (no doubt) placed their hopes
upon a pact of Collective Security
with the hidden face of the moon:
The original author of that radio play (H. G. Wells) washed his hands
surgically clean
from the social repercussions of his imaginative conception.
Bernard Shaw would not have done so.
He would have risen to such an occasion had it been given him.

Americans are still a nation of boobs (he might have said).
But Americans are more sophisticated than any other Europeans.
The so-called Europeans
who have been duped out of a United States of Europe

abandoned themselves to the delights of a war scare
under the blandishments of fact. But the dupes of the United States
of America, that land of hoax, that nation of kidders,
remained calm through the fact, and took fright
only from the creative imagination. I devoutly hope
that your great President Roosevelt
who is good enough at acting to engage in drama
will not take his cue from this experience.

But I despair to approximate the wit of a Bernard Shaw
and seek refuge in David McCord's poem from the Boston Transcript.

A TWIN TOILET, AFTER ROWLANDSON

We are almost nauseated with mulled sherry and whipped eggs.
Our barbers have filed and rubbed our nails until they are ready to bleed.
They have scraped our cheeks with humming steel
and rubbed them with milky unguents,
making us gasp with shivers down our spines.
As our valets braced their knees against our backs
to lace our stays,
we had to wedge our burning toes against the unyielding funnels
                                                        of our boots
and press our chins
against our up-standing neck bands.
They have slightly dampened our kid tights;
some smooth out the wrinkles over our bellies and thighs
while others secure our horsehair waistcoats over our ribs
with buttonhooks.
We flick a ringlet or so into place over our plucked eyebrows.
Our mirrors are most comforting, for at length our natural hair
has acquired the macaroni tone and sheen.
The butlers rub our hats along their arms, we catch
the glint of candles on our lacquered toes.
The brougham is at the door.
We fasten our gloves, we remark to one another
that they pinch our palms into anatomical semblances,

246

and as the footmen hand us our scented muffs,
that it will tax our self-restraint
to remain amused throughout the evening at Veauxhall.

from BLACKSTONE AND APPLESEED

The apple tree holds the place in New England
which the olive holds in Tuscany;
everywhere, here, north of the frost line
stand orchards, as symbols of man and labor—
lilacs as symbols of women, and of home.
The founders of the Bay Colony
took their first walk across Shawmut
and found an apple orchard
well pruned with the apple branches
like staves of baskets filled with sun,
and towards them, riding on a bull,
the apple pruner, William Blackstone.
Blackstone sold out the shares which the founders
granted him in the colony, declaring:
"I left England to get from under the Lord's Bishops,
In New England I am fallen under the Lord's Brethren."

He left Town quick and planted another orchard
in Attleboro (was it called Appleboro?),
dispensing from his retreat on Study Hill
the same kindly aloofness towards Roger Williams
and all gregarious refugees from Brethren
which he had displayed towards Robert Winthrop
and all gregarious refugees from Bishops.

King Philip exasperate from refugees and Brethren
and eremites who added orchard to orchard
burned the ten volumes of Blackstone's meditations
four days after their author died.
But the settlers of the old northwest
found apple-seedlings amid the primaeval forests

where Johnnie Appleseed, like a ghost of Blackstone,
had fled farther than the Red Tribes before them.
So are the symbols of social cultivation
and the mythical figures of solitary freedom
associated in the New England soul.

And when the hot west wind blows over Boston's Back Bay
bearing the Zion Temple's scent of the slaughter house at Brighton
Appleseed Blackstone mocks the sizzling streets.

And in the Indian Summer of Puritan Religion
Appleseed Blackstone, basking by his old Frog Pond,
saw through the squinting eyes through which alone one sees him
under the elms sedately walking
the Reverend Brahmins, Channing and Higginson.
They were ploughing through the counter tide
of merchants streaming home from counting houses.

Can one feel for these people as for one's countrymen?
We do not.

But the Paddies are country men, or city men, at least.
They settle down as they had lived here all their lives.
But every Yankee looks like a migrant bird
who has stopped for a minute on ways to parts unknown.
How do you do
                    and how do you do
                                    and how do you do
                                                    again.
One should not meet thus in haste.
We do not meet most men at all
but only their grins and the napes of their necks.
They have no time; you must understand your brethren.
They are too busy counting—What do they count?—
Beans.

In winter Appleseed Blackstone laughs at me.
I cannot escape from the Brethren . . .

As I clump down the plank walk
in our not at all very unusual New England cow-pasture
I think I hear the "L," blasting
another subway for its surface cars,
but it is only one of those indescribably dingy
indeterminately sexed outcasts
of (1) the Kipitilist Zistim (2) the Catholic and Apostolic Amalgamated,
clearing its throat.

God make speed to help us!
Lord hasten to deliver us!
We are helpless, who shall deliver us?
Deliver us from the Paddies!

"The Spring Hill Woman's Whist Party Club of St. Catherine's of Genoa's
Somerville (so says the social life columns of the *Sunday Herald*) has raised
its subscription to pay for the Mexican Onyx High Altar." Which onyx,
which altar, and indeed which church, with stations of the Cross all hand-
carved in marble, modern in style, antiqued with a tincture of kitchen tay,
a church to make four-fifths of the ramshackle shacks people go to Europe
to proclaim picturesque look like one lead dime—

Therefore do not judge the Paddies.
Judge them not, good "people of my own class,"
oh not completely, judge them not completely
on the basis of the parlourmaid—
most fortunate victim of the Kipitilist Zistim—
the parlourmaid who, in obedience to the cook,
replies to your humble request for freshly toasted
toast with the tea that "Ar, ta ba shoehurr,
and she would love to, but there has just been put
new coals on the fire,"
the while there is a sound of revelry
at five o'clock from out the deeps of the back stairs.

Judge not the Irish!
God loves the Irish!
Bridget, patron saint of Ireland,
has more Doubles of the First Class

than any other lady saint in the Calendar, saving the Blessed Virgin,
Mother of God herself, and that is
saying a great deal, it is, it is.

––––––––––––

O land without race creed color or previous condition of servitude
O land with charity for all with malice for none
O land without clean or unclean bond or free
without church or state sovereign or subject
freedom or authority law or liberty
O land without servant or master,
I am not really a soda fountain jerker. I'm just working here
until I save up enough money to be President of the USA, or something.
I made you make yourself, O land, though you did not quite get
my idea.

––––––––––––

I was in the seat behind in the railroad train
when Maria Mitchell, the mannish Nantucket astronomer,
wrote in her notebook: One peculiarity
in traveling from East to West
is that you lose the old men.
(And now the old in soul flock eastward to Boston.)
In the cars of New England you see white-headed men;
I kept one in the train up to New York
and one of greyish tinted hair as far as Erie,
but after Cleveland not a man was over forty years old.

Here if anywhere is the real America—
the greatest the richest the most prosperous
of all the great rich and prosperous
commonwealths which go to make up the mightiest
republic the world has ever seen.

O Theodore Roosevelt! here if anywhere is the real America.

Joshua made the sun stand still
but the Pope for all his Bull
could not continue its course round the Earth.

King George by royal proclamation
confined the frontiers of his colonies
but De Witt Clinton turned back
the flood of the father of waters.

There if anywhere is the real America.

Stand at Cumberland Gap
and watch the frontier pass by
on the Buffalo Trail, the Indian Trail.
Stand at South Pass and watch the frontier pass by,
the trapper's frontier, the rancher's frontier,
the farmer's, the merchant's, frontier.

There if anywhere is the real America.

Stand at Antioch, watch the frontier pass by,
Coeur de Lion's frontier, Peter the Hermit's frontier,

There if anywhere is the real America.

Americans, when from this eminence
the senses set,
forget not then whose existence
have procured to you these blessings.

(It is our aim in this school to make righteousness readable.
Children will learn without realizing that they are learning.
Teach the generation which is growing up
what democracy is and how to use it.
Teach women to successfully combine
domesticity with their business or artistic career.
The Odyssey of the average man is this:
genuine originality keeps the brain pliant.)

———————

Under the elms sedately walked
Waldo and Walt (properly Walter)
discussing literary proprieties,
defending and destroying, one afternoon, by talk and talk.

And Waldo said,
And Walt replied . . .
That day is past, and those two walk no more.

Today they hurry to their offices
—on this engaging spring day going with Appleseed Blackstone,
tickling the ribs of the giggling squirrels—
the editors of the *Atlantic*, the *Transcript*,
the *Christian Science Monitor*—
duly clean-cuffed guardians
of constructive criticism,
voices of the effectual ineffectual—
hurry to their offices.

Bring out your dead
Bring out your dead
Plague creeps over the city.

Bring out your dead, bring out your dead, the ground gives under foot.

It is a constant marvel to you that you are able to live.
One needs a world to live in. You have none,
only memorials of the past, and tangible memories
in wood and stone,
pastures punctuated by elms,
strips of sea and river shores and hills,
old ships, old flower beds, old wharves,
old arbors with their whitewash half flaked off,
the gracious discipline of hedges and brick walls—
when sudden homesickness breaks through print
or floods its radiance over collotype,
the heart leaps up, the pulse beats back a century.
You live, you are returned to your own country,
a country you know, people that know you,
people living little in memories
and less in dreams, all in days and nights,
people who live in their lives' lives—
building ships, farms, meeting houses,
ports, canals, school houses,

cities, gardens, more ships, more meeting houses—
packet lines, cotton mills, and railroad depots,
in them building a nation
and a nation within the nation, your nation.
Not this America. You have nothing to do with,
not this New England. You refuse to be a part of
this mere geographical expression.
This drag on the nation
eating its meat, burning its coal,
giving nothing, having nothing to give,
left over from the hard task of managing to stay alive.
Look at the fortunate Yankees with advantages.
These men cannot even be said to live in memories,
and surely have no dreams.
Business affords them the best vacation,
the completest rest.
Look at the unfortunate Yankee lands.
Hard work in dull towns, when no work done,
if done elsewhere, could do the national economy such harm.
People with connections worn sooner than their cheap fabrics,
a people without race, creed, color, or previous
condition of servitude;
people of the people, by the people, for the people—
Bah!
better than doughnuts.

———————

People of the North End, South End, South Boston and Revere,
good people, slightly bewildered, frazzled, but still jovial,
come, oh come, in droves and hordes,
march in a procession and deliver me,
a procession with flags and banners,
flags and standards of all nations,
coquettish, tinseled lady madonnas crowned with suns,
with moons beneath their feet, and in their hair
twelve asterisks per capita;

streamers, storms of confetti, shouts.
Beat bass drums. Come with cymbals and steam calliopes,
banjos, pianolas, saxophones, informing us

of such priceless bits of information as:
Lena is a Queen in Palestina,
Oh Mister Maeterlink, say did you never think?
Graphaphones, come oh come, and teach the Back Bay;
teach Brookline, Bay State Road, and the North Shore;
teach, if you can, Chestnut Hill and Milton; teach
all the polite environs along the Metropolitan Park System
as far as Dedham, there to meet your brothers marching
from Worcester, Fall River, Taunton,
New Bedford, Pawtucket, and Providence.
(O Bridgewater red with murdered blood!)
Teach, teach New England the necessity of life,
spill out the exuberant boiling over of the melting pot,
out over the undisturbed wilderness where no Romans came to ruin us,
a gentleness rejected by the genteel, and civilization of civility.

THE OTHER

A Theologic Dialogue

...But shut from the greater Cave of Dark and Light;
Within your cavern's dusky mouth;
Here where yes and no bear equal load
I have watched you, half an hour long,
And you do not move. What do you do?
                        Nothing.
Your eyes do not lens.   What do you think?
                        Nothing.

Have you no memories?

                        I was born in a garden.

Have you not loved?

                        My wife had beauty.

Has no one loved you?

                        I left my son.

Have you no riches?

                        I have seen a beggar.

Are you lame at heart?

                        I have looked on plague.

Are you then perfect?

                        I have looked on death.

Do you learn nothing?

                        I have meditated.

Do you never hunger?

                        I have fasted.

Do you know nothing?

                        I am not yet nothing.

What do you pray?

                        I cannot pray.

But pray then. Pray to the Sky that streams
Around with its quiet Wheel of Stars
Never stepping out of Order to the Zenith;—
Some always sinking while the others are rising;
None ever straying from the Company of Planets,
Who never limp from their different Order.

Can you not pray to the Sky that sends our Seasons
To cut the melon Years apart in Halves and Quarters?
Pray to the Stars!
              Large hulks reach limits,
              the sky must stream,
              the stars wheel;
              I don't see the infinite in these.
Yes; but pray then to the Sun's life-flaming blaze
Round whom this Zodiac, in the Milky Way
Journeys every Year across the Sky;
And to whom daily even unliving Rock
Acknowledges attendant Heat. Light and warmed
Life of worms and every limber growth,—
Life, Light, and Sun, who are one in their Nature,—
Pray to these.
              No, for light comes from the sun;
              life comes from light.
              I would be less than death:
              I live; and so long as I live
              I cannot pray to life.
Yes; but pray then to the Moon whose gleams
Guide the alternate tides of Life and Death
Whose ebb and flood gleam deathly;
Or laud the dark, dumb slumber of Light.
Pray then to Death!
              No: all dark turns light;
              nor can one learn to die
              by libations to death.
Yes; but pray the unborn, elemental
Flaxen Earth whence you arose, and whither,
With deathless seeds, you sink to stir
Withered Earth, who pulls us towards
Those Desires, felt by all Worlds,
Which hold them lariat.
              No; for all worlds are tombs;
              the crushed seed dies;
              so scatter the sterile
              ash of burnt-out jars.
Porphyry-born Waters (which are Ice and Steam,

256

From which your Body and your Mind are made)
Hold you in their Hands, local, between two Deaths'
Erodent streams, whose laving waves remain.
                    Water reflects my image;
                    the image wavers.
Yes; but then to the Air (whose never-resting
Waves move not, whose breath is ours)
Pray; and to Winds, whose ways are the Law of Souls.
Laud this Air, the Atlas who lifts sound;
And that Charon, who ferries rarer Azure
Speed of instant Lights from Star to Star.
                    No. Would you have me pray
                    with my own breath to my own voice?
Fire consumes all, like your hand-over-head
Consuming Reason. Fire, to create all,
Desolates things. To Fire and to consuming,
Creating Reason,—pray to these.
                    And after reason destroy
                    scarlet destruction;
                    how, then, pray?
Yes, praise. Praise whole Parabolas
Of Time and Space (lisping, shell-dark lanes)
For openings in Chaos where (past evil Mysteries) each
Free Miracle of our minds may leak and leach
Through folded mesh of Fate and Stars.
                    No; but I have heard:
                    five senses and unnumbered sense
                    listen subliminal and always
                    to threshold voices beyond space;
                    and these voices say:—nothing.
                    If having heard is praise, I pray.
Yes, but pray first. Live in prayer. Prayer is act;
Act, prayer. Listen less tensely;—hear the Tetragram
—(Yod. He. Vau. He.)—
Not made, Perfect; but linked in all
Air and Cloud and Heat and Stone
Instantly from blank facture all. Praise
Humid Dark and solid Light,
Liquid Fire-Letters for the Word's

Wind of numb ice, consuming void.
Hymn motion and labor and lives of Things thought-to-live:
Eagle and winged Lion and Bull and Man;
Fish, Phoenix, Lamb, and Pelican; or
Hammer, and Lash, and Sponge, and Lance; or
Thorns, and Tree; and Corn and Wine.
      No; and what need for prayer
      if such be used aright?
      Such piety implies impiety.
Yes; but men pray because hardy use requires
Praise of the work of men's hands;
So pray the Persian's Zoroastrian Fires;
Praise Image, Apollonian, of Hellene or Hindoo,
Whose Wills from their helpless Symbols generate
Processes from tomb or idol. In Compassion
Shut their Lares up together, placate them, guard
Against robbers of Good Use, and robbers of the Word.
      No; and a guardsman lord himself
      greater (and lesser) than his treasure-heap?
Yes, but the most lean, savage tolerance
Of Heathens who invade their Imaginations
Witnesses against you who fake aloof long-sighted
Ignorance of habit, custom, circumstance.
The humbled Word is housed in decent things
To emerge hesitant in decent acts
By washing blames and healing smarts and Harm.
Are you so innocent of the Trance
Through which the Bride follows the Bridegroom's dance?
      No. And if one knew such,
      one could do such.
      How does one know?
Yes, but I know; because I pray. Pray and know how I know
The known World's seen and unseen flower
Whose likely Order breathes out odor
Of unknown, unmoved, but moving Power.
      No; and I pray to an ideal,
      I shall see all things fail.
Yes, but the Father's Laborant
(Hovering—beyond Time—over lymph, hueless Unction

Of all, from nought, to some, Instant)
Forms all things handily; and finds all things function.
            No; and your coeval, seeing spirit
            (if not the evil-leering devil
            who made humans wise to evil)
            knowing us devoid of merit,
            on a day of wrath and mourning
            knew the evil we inherit.
Yes, but the God of Love became man's lad
To help man, that man might live with God;
Whose willed complacency to man's sad
Death, allows to man that God is Man, in God.
            No, and to change the loathful hate
            to live, who willed your loved one's fate
            show man that god is god-in-man.
Yes, but I ask not why evil hampers a work which Perfect
Power made perfect. Say not: "To lug good out of evil";
But tell me true. If you know,—I shall never pray.
            No; and I have so little
            knowledge;
            I ask not why, but how.
            Mist and the dark
            ring lamps never so wide.
Yes, but we know enough: Man scuttles Nature.
But the Lodestone (good to Evil cold
As Cold is emptied of all Heat)
Plumbs Tides of Pride
And hinges Nature to its Magnet Pole.
            No; you for your soul
            Wed your evil;
            and for your father
            kiss your devil.
But how did He hearten us, liven
Our Ape-like Spirits and bodies that flatter Death,
Even by suffering our Spirit and our Flesh?
Calm Sufferer, who did away with Wrath
Suffering your Passion's Sacrifice, I am shriven
From my Death and return initiate, sworn into Heaven.
            And I; and me; and mine

not to return were more repentant.
As we handle outward things,
so is one inwardly.
Compassion all things, pity none;
nor judge between man and the world.
None feel hang-dog guilt who know
nothing evil, nothing good.
Yes you, like a woman jealous of a painting,
Scorn the niche (yes, however poor the niche):
Bitch eyes are shallower for blame of the framed treasure.
No, and this mystery's evil origin
discloses little of the facts of sin.
Having harbored evil well, I offer now
my suffering with your like, for all but him
I loathe who lent your sufferers suffering.
If, as you say, priest, victim, god are one,
the sacrifice, made foolish, is undone.
But it was Man killed God. Man. Yes, you!
(All in the Name of your Decorum's Ends.)
See with me how the Evil, planted, grew;
For I (a Man) am (like my God) a Jew;—
And it was I killed God, I before you.
(And all in His ten-fold negative Commands).
My race, in desert drouth, found the desert Lord,
A Jealous God who will be served alone;
(The God heard in the Ear and heard Abroad).
He made and judges all from His Power's throne
Who proved my Race the Nation of the Law,
By errors tried, peculiarly His own.
The God of Power, to make his People proud,
Oppressed them by all Powers of the Earth;
Lent them Bard and Hero, whom they scorned and stoned
In preparation for his own lonely Birth.
We are transcendant from that trampled Nation
Of graceful Egypt Heir and your sceptic East,
Yet chiefly Heir of their strange Destiny
To stand aside from India and Greece
With patent of approximate Prophecy.
Then Prophets save but by full Revelation

To so near as ravening Nature comes to Man
So near, no nearer, to the Godhead's feast
Come Natural Men who feed on the God-Man.
Else, why did not the Elemental Word
Enter only the Elements, or enter
Noble Trees or Rocks; the Worms and Ants;
The Crocodile or Tortoise, Hen, Adder, Cobra;
The Bat, the Vulture, Ibis, Hawk and Raven?
Jackal, Hyssop, Lynx, Hyena,
Any good Animal, the Cat, the Dog;
Hogs, Wolves or Tigers; Seal or Whale,
Bees, Leek, Garlic, Elephant, or Onions?

      And you hear not your word in these,
      then the humbug humdrum
      you hear in man is not the word.
      And if you ponder long on hearsay puzzles,
      you are no servitor to needs.
      In need, the word is linear;
      it has no need for nearer-come,
      nor Teachers made lazy by their riddles
      who frustrate matyrdom.

Yes, but Beaver, Rat, Squirrel, Dolphin, or the fruited
Shoots of sea-flowers, flowers of weed and rice;—
All these observe their Fates and shame our Pride,
Whose lot is to be proud. We who divide
Beasts from beast, Clean and unclean, and our Race
From other races, Day from days; we uproot
Month from months, and turn Temple to a larder-house,
Make Temples out of dull schoolrooms; and drive
Our Spirits into brain, our bellies into Nerve.
On Sinai's mortar slabs of Thou Shalt Not,
The ember berries of Midian's burning bush
Let loose we crush into a mash, and squeeze the verve
Juices and mix in bitter Wine.

      Men build stone walls
      against winds of their gods
      from the god's laws of stone.
      Under our shadow-gods we crawl
      lizards to stone from light.

> Light makes stone-gods and lizard-worms shadow;
> dark alone holds no shade.

Yes, but a Light opposed to your doubt's Light
Melts all Jew thought to mock but Rote and Rita
Seeing man lives for God, not God for men,
We quiet Sorrow under skies of ash
Vengefully stirring tribal Wrath;
And find synod and Synagogue, the rebukes and glories
Among all races, hold Race no more,
Priestdom no longer; our Tribes, scummed from all Powers
Fled to all, in every tribe and in all Nations' stories
Haunt through sad commentaries on History;
Levite lineage, honoring old Lore, outrages ours,
And moulding unseen Idols from Poetry,
On fissured altars immolates Prophecy.

> No; why water, year by year,
> a blasted shrub
> which bears no fruit,
> which leaves, but flowers no more?

I do not. On the dead Tree of Law
(As God hangs on the Limbs of Death) my Grapevine
Draws from all soil and loam an equal nutriment;
Hung on its shoots, ripened Grapes ferment
Its tender Roots, which split all Rock asunder,
Are tended by the Gardener of Thunder.
For Lucifer (Morning Star of Heaven)
Is a Light no longer (having slipped and dropped).
In the Pit his falling lit and left, the New Day Star
Planted His Seed. And this Grapevine springs
Where Stars may dance and Birds level their wings.
And those who eat its Grapes, inebriate
Hear Voices of dead Saints, Heroes to come,
Heroes not dead, and Voices of their Fate
Singing, as Reapers lilt their Harvest Home.
From the Grapevine, Queen, all Rods and Crowns are given;
And Kings lean eagerly for the Sword-Key she brings;
And she shall lift their Swords against these Kings;
And rule all Space to close or unclose Heaven.
She is the new Creation, this fierce Vine

262

Whose Grapes are Peace, and whose spilled Wine
Is War . . . .
> Panoplied in lion skin
> long might an ass crop
> tender green barley-shoots;
> but his bray is his ruin.

Yes; but the Church, the Bride of God;
All men's handmaid and bride, their Mother-
Love (which flows from Slayer and from Slain)
Speaks (like the birds) auricular tongues of man
In unison with that lithe Immaculate Lover
Who bore the Incomprehensible's longing
And gave the Word birth through her obedient womb.
> No; and how was she punished,
> poor listless lewd?
> For the first time the devil
> lazed behind woman's dress
> her liege and children called her evil,
> reviling her for their own nastiness.
> Did I hear the chain of a manacle?

Each bore the other's pain, so that the Birth was peaceful
Like the flooding of light over a peaceful dawn.
(This is wrought by the blending of terrible elements)
And as the Birth of Jesus was the beginning of His Death
We may learn how the sacrifices of our lives are not always painful;
But that the most serene and peaceful times of our existence
Are a part and parcel of the universal Passion
As is the case with peaceful nations and periods of civilization,
The fruits and earnings of expended pain and turmoil.
But the Mother of Jesus Immortal, Maiden eternal,
Gracious; listed above all blest; I tell
Her Prayers whose paps fed Forgiveness
Who (when He grew and left her, wept when he wept) suffered
His agonies and Death; dry-eyed bathed His Dead Head;
And bitterly lamented.
> Do the blest fear, and flee for safety;
> do the gracious mourn and grieve;
> or find it so dolorous to be hard-by perfection;
> do they tell of sorrow;

263

or the uprooting of sorrow?
Yes; but continually we tell Memory of God's Death
And (throughout Time) reentry into Life;
Who in the night in which He was betrayed
Took bread;
And wine; gave thanks; broke; poured;
And said:
This is My Body, This My Blood,
This do.
This we praise; and this we take
Hand to mouth and Holy
Immense in majesty, honorable in comfort;
Deliverers, victors, final judges;
Helpful servants, secure heritage;
Governors extolled and worshipped;
Lured always away from error;
Pitiful, fruitful, never confounding
Good wealth of well-willed men;
We praise; we bless; we worship; we thank;
We give mercy and receive mercy;
This we think and this we take; this only is holy.
Our daily lunch repeats (like a moth's larval ghost)
Identically one sufficient Death.
In this seven-times pregnant Sacrament,
Our Bowels cleave to Bread, made living Flesh;
God lives in His Elect, who live upon His Host.
Their Sin is offal; Life His nutriment.
                         No, and sinner-saint
                         breathe in blame by one link,
                         god, by self-cruelty were slain,
                         (what is that clink
                         of chain?),
                         but that your cruelty towards him
                         lynches him to life again.
                         He saved himself; and you cannot save?
His Body, with no Death-Germ in all its cells,
Heaved deep, plunged down, and sunk in the Death-laded
Tank of the Night-Font; shivered it all with bright
Waves which lap their Obedient, whom Baptism

Wakens from loaf of living to work out in God's Will.
This is not yesterday's heat caught in a chilly house,
This the Fountain (not the Tank) of Faith
Whose welling Issues heal fissures of Schism
Gashed between Fact and Truth in the World's tissues.

        Your hidden, latent priest
        (as a butcher, his shackled beast
        cleaves and laves)
        has what-he-will with his own, and cleaves
        soul uncreated into many souls
        huddled all together into one sink of blood.

Yes, but to that hard Messianic Judge, start and end and all,
I pray: Come soon; Return; Breathe aloud to melt the rotted snow.
High Wind, blow—endlong, hollow—sea to sea;
O Flame to burn the Law; O Key to unlatch jail in
Orient dawn desire to remould Earth;
Long-drawn, come; Deliver the People,
Visit the Wicket; Make straight haste; stand among us;
Judge, stand among us at hand, in lull, set up your Help:
Come along and let us be happy, let us ask for all
We like,—alacrity is already set. O you only thorough spring thaw,
Though the hard-pan barrens lift brief argument
"Are you the one? Must we not look for another?"
You only are the thorough spring thaw.
Winter shaken, the reeds lurch flat before your haste;
The frozen headwaters of sense hash open:—
Dumb, Deaf, blind Lunes, lump Cripples lope and dance,
Cowards see Vengeance take up arms
and blast thieves clean out (long past time).
Lift your eyes up, now, to the way it comes ahold
Allelulia! Hellow! Halloo! Look it is here:
Fig trees curl their harsh buds in, under lush clouds,
To fruit by thousands alert through endless spring!

        No; and how you do love a lord!
        All season and all kingdom end.
        This blare bugler must levet again,—
        is not almighty: ever striving,—
        cannot judge; knowing evil,—
        is not finished.

Who wield Power?
What makes Perfect?
Did you hear a clank-clinking
Manacle?

> They are not perfect and it is not one;
> the no beginning and no end I see
> of knowledge where all thoughts dissolve;—
> They need not men, but men have passionate
> need of them, who neither live nor die;
> who have not power, nor weakness, but sufficiency;—
> no ignorance, nor forgetfulness;
> and without ledgered number hold the same;
> unformed, unknowable, without defect,
> in act or in not acting; with no name;
> without adversary, and opposed to nothing;
> and know not anger; being not opposed,
> nor dead.

Yes, but get Dead;
And again Natal,
—Full Statured—
Immortal!

> No (and hear that chained manacle?)
> who leave their names on a latrine wall,—
> such wish names on the scroll of life.
> Your resurrection from the dead
> to your world-to-come is a new fall.
> The cups of the mill-wheel descend
> which, with drowning god-selves, you ascend
> churning the burning hell in which you would dissolve.

Surgeon and Surgeon's knife keep up
Intent
Although the Patient die.
Give up
Life to gain Life—
Aesculapian Covenant
Contract of Surgery.

> At a sour close of hunt or battle
> does a surgeon moan: "Before I pull
> this arrow out, I would lief tell

who wounded you: his height; class; home; color;
king; servant; priest; or householder;
short, or of mean height; or tall?"
(Braves turned brave to save their lives
will not stay brave when their alone life fail)
Would anyone half dead by such an arrow stay
his surgeon's healing, asking: "Answer, Say
is the bowstring milkweed? with shaft of vulture
feathers and wound with monkey sinews;
the arrow a claw-head, iron claw a calf's tooth?"
This latter were long dead before he learned;
those former, forever damned before immortal.

Jesus' Heirs Christ's Legacy inherit:
O the dreadful Physician does not leave us dreary
(Though the Transfigured Christ—Whole Normal Man—
Leaves half hearts a hollow Lacune while not there).
"To cure bodily ill, heal ills of Spirit"
Is prescribed in Jesus' secret Medicine.
While, like long-robes, we heckled round His Grave's Lair
Poor quack Patients and shyster Clients ferret
Out Jesus' Crimes and Disease (any Law can);
Though we make a Code of Christ's alegal Merit
To end up with as little Faith as we began),
He (opening Doors yet unopened) breathes: "Open,
Christ Church, to me Real Presence,—near, as far as near."

Yes, but the history
of your chosen race
hints of the future
for your holy church.

Yes, but though Hell Gate may prevail
Against Christ's handful till Christ come again,
Whereas Sects leave their lech behind them, dead,—
Deader than limace which hoddy land-snails peel
Or a seashell where crabs scorn to dwell;
Christ Church, His new Creation for His new Elect
(Though, like the old, it havoc Reason) alone
Shall hunt His Saints up (while it persecute)
In Tribe and City (as hostage Truth repel
Hostile Contradictions) Christ Church

(though it hit at every job besides its own)
In no age leaves the Mission in the lurch
In any season, Gospellers' gospel:
We do not lust; nor lie; nor counterfeit
Our word; nor envy. We honor our Elders; we are kind.
(Did you hear that clinking grate of manacle?)
We do to others as we would have others do,
And hence: Whose Sins remitted, are remit;
But whose Sins We retain,—they are retained.

                    No; but their pardon does not forgive
                    your pardon's limit,
                    nor your forgiveness
                    their lack in forgiveness. Tell,
                    what if another cannot
                    wish just what you wish?
                    I see the briar and thorn you pull
                    you lap and bundle into faggot.

Yes; but we leave good after us as we race
About; we heal the sick; we tell the Truth; we love
And therefore are loved, and killed. Yet feeling our dull
Names graven by Faith, we open them in Hope.
Most unlike other men, but most like Man, with Zeal
To tell forth God's Good News; and we embrace
The Desert, and refuse foods, powers, and fames.

                    No? and Greed? Does God then feel
                    some lech for these? I am not rude . . .
I am glad you told me.

                    I am puzzled, having never seen
                    through highways down byways
                    any slaughtering of men who heal.
                    But priests, who love the alms of poverty
                    (which transcends all horse sense),
                    why are priests hewed down by the poor
                    (their nursery of innocence)?
                    Do priests in the name of "sacrifice"
                    (with their complacent stance)
                    oblate the plagues of ignorance?
The blame of Ministers are no blame of Ministry:
And could its Ministers deny the Word

Yet in their speaking it, the Truth is spoken;—
(Not thought, more true; but Truth, God's end
Truth—not the better-thought—but Good).
Though the Church sin (being Human), the Innocent
Sufferers for its Virtue by its Sin
Are lesser Types of Christ. Their repeated deaths repent
Us Christ's brave Death, their singular Origin.
With names below Roll-Calls of the leet Wise,
They yet hold chairs in Heaven's parliament,
Of our private lives public Confessional.
(Whence came that sound of clinking manacle?)
And they allege: "Forgive" as each, final, is sent
Before the head-court tribunals of the last Assize.

                    No and all these last
                    things happen in you
                    whereon all worlds base.
                    If your god cannot give all level place
                    he is lower than you
                    and teases men into libbers
                    and blandly limes their women,
                    himself each and the same
                    hermaphrodite half-seas-over.
                    Making one soul wish not to die,
                    he makes many wish not to live.
                    In what too much do you believe?
                    Did ever so deep a doubt in life
                    make for so limpid clear
                    a hankering after death?
                    Rehearse me over your death-creed and lore,
                    I shall recall you your life-prayer.

But I believe in God, my Father, the Unknowable
Creator of Heaven and Earth.
                    And who makes this name holy
                    on earth, as in heaven?
But my Brother God, who suffered the Father's
Forgiveness; crucified; dead; buried.
                    And can his commune come
                    on earth, as in heaven?
But in their Spirit God, Over-Lord over life

Who speaks through un-tongued Prophets.
                    And is the will ever done
                    on earth, as in heaven?
But by that one Death which expurges Sin.
(May Light perpetually shine upon you.)
                    And not by our daily bread as we
                    forgive on earth, as in heaven?
But in tenure to repented Dead
(May Light perpetually shine upon us.)
                    And never be led from temptation
                    on earth, as in heaven?
But with dead Flesh living from the Grave.
(May Light perpetually shine upon them.)
                    And then, how be delivered from evil
                    on earth, as in heaven's hallow-tide?
But through the pull toward ended Sacrifice
And the Kingdom and the Power and the Glory.
                    And kingdom and power and glory
                    world without end
                    on earth, as in heaven?
No; but heckler,
Haggle, wreck, hack and limb the Faith
(Life's lathe and scaffold),
What Virtue is left built?
                    None can ever be built;
                    simple, divine
                    virtue is heavy search:
                    right will, right act,
                    right thought, and choice;
                    right word, and end;
                    right memory, right faith.
Yes but spiral to lofts of Faith from the loobs of Hell's
Hole by our Sacrament's seven bridges of metals
Resmelted to Soul and Matter's prime alloy.
Not that I hold to the long lode; but do you, Lector,
Hold hard and fast to eight divided mutuals?
                    No. Nor do I
                    to my lectures. Why?
                    Why do you cry?

May I cry for you . . . and me?
                    Yes. But don't cry.
No, I shall turn, turn to the mouth of the cavern.
Thence now comes the noise of clinking manacles.
                    What did you tell
                    of this serving man who climbs
                    to you, loaded with your chains?
Yes, too much, but not enough; for you
Who deny my God point out my Lord to me.
                    Yes, but he is your twin.
                    Go. But look back on me.
No, I shall see you but as you were before.
Enough. Let up. Handsome enemy, call it off.
Your brave questions bang the Soul's grave gong.
                    And friend, your lancinate answers
                    pierced me with poison.
                    I was immune to its hallucination
                    but yet it kindled
                    all my life's unlined and tangled
                    delusions into labyrinth dream illusion.
Yes, to build
Dream intention out of life,
Asleep to sin
Awake in Righteous.
                    No, but to tell half-truths in the name of truth
                    half asleep, woken; awake while dreaming;
                    to play dead, living; and with day after night.
                    Yes, let's halt now, and turn to that seeming
                    behind you god's face being
                    man's halo. Follow. Turn, friend,
                    towards the sound of clinking manacles.
                    There the hum-rumbles of the bright
                    world hushes the mouth of my hall's vocal stone.
                    Here Yes and No have equal weight.
                    Go. Let me lease. Leave me alone.
                    Go. Fuse with my thought in effort to refute
                    within that huger cave of dark and light.
                    Let your twin lock your left hand in his chain.
But you half and half blasphemer, do I see

your dispassionate Blasphemy
allude the hints of God?
                              And you and your twin's benignant enmity
                              melt mirror to mirror without trace?
Yes and, as I turn, I have seen three
Handfast, allied reflections, Face to Face.

INDEX

INDEX OF TITLES AND FIRST LINES

275

A16 90

Composition and printing of this edition
of fifteen hundred copies were accomplished by
Stamperia Valdonega in Verona, Italy.
JUNE MCMLXXII